BLOSSOMING

BLOSSOMING

DHARMA DIARY POEMS

VOLUME II

by

JOY MAGEZIS

BLACK
APOLLO
PRESS

First published in Great Britain by Black Apollo Press, 2012
Copyright © Joy Magezis
The moral right of the author has been asserted.
A CIP catalogue record of this book is available at the
British Library.
ISBN: 9781900355742

To my dear
life partner, Bob
Without you
this wouldn't be possible

To my children
Kerin and Kevin
Granddaughters
Sophie and Ella

To entire human family
such interconnection
May peace and love
Blossom for us all

CONTENTS

INTRODUCTION

Five years of poems
since last collection
Experiencing so much
Such chance to grow

Amazing travel
Nowhere to get to
Inner exploration
Vivid outer world

Interconnected
seen through perceptions
As vision clears
heart-shine expands

Sun breaks after storm
Birds fly from bare tree
Taking in this beauty
Alive this instant

Inviting you to join me
through these realisations
Perhaps this will nourish
your own journey

Smiling to you now
Thank you my friend
for sharing this poem
May your peace blossom wide

14 January 2012, Cambridge UK

2 February 2007

Preparing to leave Further Education College teaching after seventeen years

Life shifts in progress
Shocking, though expected
Suddenly I'm old
Retiring at 60

Pension papers galore
Explain your life, Joy
How can I prove
what agency deleted?

I can't remember dates
over 20 years ago
I want to be honest
But fair to myself

Fear of small pension
with mind less clear
All I can do
is fill in best I can

Meditation, Reiki
will help me preserve
clarity of mind
Or at least lessen fear

Reiki comes through
bringing new client
Training I desire
showing possibilities

Book being typeset
David thorough, kind
Drawings soften
inner angst revealed

Here in my centre
deep belly tells
that I'm vulnerable
Though more solid

Be kind to self, Joy
with difficult demands
Feel wonder surround
as grace resonates

With mind shift
away from clinging
Birdsong is clearer
Sunlight streams through

16 February 2007

Arrival at my door of freshly published first volume of my poems, entitled The Universe for Breakfast

Wondrous arrival
of my dharma book
with perfect cover
sweet, clear drawings
Comfortable with poems

Amazing happening
Unexpected
though anticipated
Recycling past terror
insight, transformation
into newborn book

So long in gestation
over eight years of poems
chosen and proofed
Written for my healing
through such deep sorrow
Joyous reconnections

After such long labour
then arrives the birth
There in my hands
purple lotus cover
soft, off-white pages
Words in new form

So grateful and amazed
Lemons into lemonade
New look of my trials
Beauty walks on green
Love of family
Compassion for self

Marking near end
of phase of my life
I still fear turning 60
asking for pension
trusting own powers
Allowing healer bloom

Money problems loom
as does great adventure
Faith in myself
to manage both
and let it all go
so life can unfold

20 February 2007

Approaching 60
Party lurking
Details spin
Just breathe, smile

Body aging
feeling tired
Resistance noted
to March 3rd

Reiki student
oh, so sweet
Pleased to share
life force wisdom

Want more promo
change web, leaflet
Increase prices
with concession

Hard to have
lazy day
Inhale ease
Enjoy projects

Yet dread lingers
to next weekend
Smile and note
That's alright

Want to give
me the gift
of permission
to just be

Thay says
be creative
Walks mindfully
because he likes it

Confucius said
when he was 60
did heart's desire
without breaking precepts

Sister says
greatest freedom
just to see
whatever's there

Process, process
you are here
to help me grow
into Cronehood

*   *   *

Kev rings happy
Ella is one
Oh, such *naches*
Shinning connection

Beautiful family
Intimate energy
shared together
Photos I sent

Heart opens wide
We chat of year ago
Time so quick
This day special

All my fear
of party vanishes
In spirit of love
friends will share joy

14

4 March 2007

After book launch birthday party

Being 60
cool, light
Satisfied

Party warmth
family, friends
joyful smiles

Book reading
Heart touching
feeling depth

Freely dedicating
Warm relations
Signing books

Vietnam exhibit
Smile surround
Devotional link

Lunar eclipse
grey moon cover
turning red

May this shift support me
in moving past guilt victim
into third age vision

8 March 2007

International Women's Day

Yesterday savouring
closeness with Bob
Him leaving for States
Me getting senior card

At college celebrating
International Women's Day
Women's class speaks
of war women suffer

We come together
from so many lands
Holding hands
Ushering peace

15 March 2007

Pension less than they said
Something about opting out
More phone calls to pursue
as I breathe through fear

I do feel stable and sure
Universe breathing through me
We have always survived
Mindfulness now builds future

Last night's sit so deep
Sangha sharing through
tangles of guilt I saw
but was still caught in

Making way for this morning
finding pension letter shock
Accepting outcomes will unfold
beyond my expectations

Loving myself as is
trusting whatever happens
I'll find way to deal with it
Opening my heart to light

Finding the balance between
greed and needing to survive
Wanting comfortable old age
through wise, ethical life

When I'm entangled in guilt
I lose the clarity of vision
Precepts are there to follow
Interpretation not always clear

And I am not Confucius
never breaking precepts at 60
while allowing heart's desire
Though I do make a real effort

Suffering caused by my cows
Yet need to defend myself
A balance still hard to find
Allow life's lessons to appear

Beyond condemnation
I can better grow
Embracing insecurity
Precepts not made for guilt

Wear your sword
as long as you can
to see what's comfortable
and what seems right

Today the sky is blue
River slowly flows on
Reflecting life as it is
Wondrous beauty aglow

9 May 2007

After a retreat of the Order of Interbeing, the core community of Zen Master, Thich Nhat Hanh, called 'Thay' by his students (which means teacher in Vietnamese).

Glimpsing Universe surround
more than just this body
Remembered, reconnected
after touching earth
with my OI Sangha

Rediscovered, reblooming
of what I already know
covered with worry illusion
masking my true essence
shinning back through fog

Sense beyond seeing
horizontal through head
across third eye
temples opening to feel
this oneness bursting smile

Smile to Order Members
walking meditation on route
past wood we carry fuel
to light the bonfire
around which we sing

Serenading the flames
built high with orange light
Meditating with open eyes
I watch the crackling dance
Smoke drifting to dense stars

I am one with this moment
darkness twinkling with light
Trust building as we walk
guiding elder back
Mara great teacher in being

Remember as I return
to life's ups and downs
beauty being more than body
joy in essence surround
vivid flowers in my garden

10 May 2007

Healing past hurts
within and without
Source of discomfort
wants soft, pink mist

Hunt for missing child
Suspicion fuels the fear
compounding negative spin
Touching our nightmare

There in depth of fright
inner child screams in pain
Dread thick enough to smell
seeks love-cloud comfort

Ease of being whole
one with universe
Allows loosening
to touch and hold our pain

Light streams through
shining on knifepoint
sticking painfully in
soft underbelly

Release is a *mechaieh*
reconnecting sweet solace
So confidence can smile
to let forgiveness grow

If Ian Paisley and Martin McGuinness
could together form a government
Then Northern Ireland peace process
shows us reconciliation way

Oh, the hope of all people
family misunderstandings
Shine with peace process light
igniting understanding

8 June 2007

After Phung taught the Cambridge Sangha community some Vietnamese recipes, which was the start of what grew into the Vegetarian Vietnamese Cookery book.

Sharing cultures, cooking
with my Sangha friends
Savouring our mix
both sweet and tart

Vegetarian ingredients
from Asia and Britain
Bring a new generation
of Fusion Cooking

Richness of our temple
at Phung and Phuoc's home
Phuoc says house not theirs
just using for this generation

Their ancestors look on
as ours join in as well
English, Welsh, Irish
Russian-Jewish, German

Cambridge Sangha warmth
rotating facilitators
meeting at each other's
Building mindful awareness

Fundraising for Vietnamese kids
as we learn flavourful cooking
Phung so wise and skilled
passes on grandmother's ways

Lessons give me confidence
to expand my repetoire
Together we joyfully eat
Savouring what we share

8 June 2007

SOPHIE'S SWEET BEAN CAKE

Four year old granddaughter joins us
for the start of Vietnamese cooking
We mix up bean cake together
stirring in coconut, sugar

Sophie laughs and giggles
She sings *Round and Round*
Watches cake cook in oven
sitting high up on stool

Waiting, Sophie does gymnastics
But when cake comes out of oven
she suddenly sits quietly at table
Sucking fingers in anticipation

Yes, she enjoys the taste
is happy to take some home
We marvel later eating cake
how delicious is Sophie's laugh

Tree Introductions
with book in hand
Anna and I
go out to meet them

What are your names
I have wondered
on so many walks
on Stourbridge Common

Ash, grouped thin leaves
Willow, like weeping
Poplar, chiming friend
communing with hug

Sycamore, helicopter seeds
London Plane, spotted bark
Both remind me of Maples
I saw in New Jersey

Alder, pine cones
Elder, white flowers
Lime, thin leaf at fruit
Hawthorn in garden

Horse Chestnut
Collected conkers
with children
when young

Such fun looking deeply with Anna
Suddenly I can remember names
Exciting to share with Bob
Introductions bring us closer

14 June 2007

Kilburn farewell party
for college building axed
Attracting old timer friends
who helped me get the job

Gerry, my Head of English
held discussions, took votes
Kathy's Language Support
Together brought in change

From place of respect
for lecturers and students
positive energy flowed
allowing diversity to flourish

Need to teach standard English
while valuing other versions
Gerry leading visualisations
for relaxation and clarity

What a change of college culture
What changes have come within me
bringing such massive growth
deepening understanding, compassion

Pain of involuntary redundancy
cutting deep into valuing staff
Overshadowing touching reunion
with so many old colleagues

So nice to see them anyway
rekindling our mutual past
Ginger, Beatrice, Heather
Ann, Diana and Pete

Sharing our struggles together
doing best we could for students
Roger, Mike reminiscing success
students going to Uni or jobs

Knowing we touched their lives
gave students confidence, fresh start
Unskilful management handling
can never negate their triumphs

As we savour that success
feel our deep accomplishments
May Principal, Personnel open heart
in clarity to rethink their actions

Sadness of Women's Studies demise
though course was validated
But that created space for Reiki
allowing me to prepare to leave

20 June 2007

Celebrating Women's Courses
ending after fifteen years
of teaching in various forms
Opening my heart, helping women

Feeling so good at the finish
of Women Into Computing
The end of an era for me
End of an era for college

Touching warmth of affection
from women's grateful thanks
How much confidence they gained
Knowledge beyond expectations

Pat and I feel satisfied
seeing all they learnt
Knowing we've done well
whatever happens at college

3 July 2007

***I read this at my last departmental meeting,
as no party was held for those of us leaving.***

Ode to College of North West London
Old Kilburn College transformed
Second building torn down behind me
This time I'm walking away
but needed housing'll spring up

I remember early days at South Kilburn
writing on blackboard with dusty chalk
Suddenly wondering what I was doing
then turning round to find
earnest refugees hungry for English
How could I disappoint them?

Yes, it's the students who taught me
shaped me into their teacher
told me of their cultures
deepened me with their life stories
Showed me the power of courage

And there's been all those women
from Women in Computing and beyond
to Women's Studies, Return to Learning
empowered by shift in perspective
Seeing how cards stacked against them
could be turned round through understanding

Colleagues were my support
working together through chaos
Running one week ahead
or teaching same year after year
Discussing those difficult students
and many who made us proud

Shocking to retire after 17 years
though I've planned it for quite a while
I haven't wanted to leave with anger
though redundancies have tested my resolve
I'm saddened at unskilful senior managers
The system eclipsing their humanity

I want to wish everyone well
sending my hope for a future
where the cycle comes back round
to valuing students and staff
with time and space to be unique

Beyond paperwork to essence
of what we all believe
that learning changes lives
in second chance FE
We know we make a difference

Just found out Brent Archive will take
all those women's books and papers
Though women's courses all cut
their history will be preserved
to help light a path to the future

As for me, I'll keep writing
My book of poems has come out
I'll be teaching Reiki healing
Treating patients with care
And what I learnt at college
will keep growing within

24 July 2007

Written in Salema, Portugal on holiday
with my beloved life partner, Bob

Getting intimate
with the sea
Immersed, we are one
turquoise and green
rippled by wind

Only two minutes
of quick movement
to get the body warm
Fingers can take longer
but it's always worth it

Breathing in freshness
Out breath release
all those city worries
Watching slabs of time
melt back into sand

Swimming by shoreline
people look in wonder
the water seems so cold
But I'm warm and homey
in sync with life source

Water within, without
this form we call 'body'
I am a part of ocean
back to true birthplace
being larger me

29 July 2007

Pink moon rising over Salema bay
Stripes of white waves rush to shore
Brighter as it rises so round and full
Smiling face within

Difficulties pass in vast sea
now streaked with soft light
turning orange against blue
Such beauty surpasses mundane

In the growing darkness
moon trail comes to me
turning intense white
entering my heart
Path expands aglow
illuminating waves

Remembering Mom's painting
Being here with her
Meditating with moon
solidity restored
Confidence returns

Now stars harmonise
Crickets chirp their song
I breathe with the moon
She's deep in heart

Burning through despair
as boat crosses path
shining small search light
slowly moving on

Hands on chest centre
feeling energy there
'Oooh,' we both say
We are steady, free

7 September 2007

Non-Joy elements unite
reforming for new start
Allowing me to re-phase
to shape my world again

College lecturer no more
Needing space to breathe
Connect with stepping feet
on earth's resonation

Vibrating through me
life force energy
Bringing parts together
in greater, clear whole

Term started without me
as I babysat for Kev
Combing Ella's hair
Bonding time together

Essential baby being
eating, changing nappies
Playing with puppets
Freshness anew

Ordination before
warmth of friends on path
Collective consciousness
nurtures transformation

Letting go of fear
Understanding, deepening
Allowing myself to heal
come into new time

Slate so white and empty
Opening for beginnings
to take only what I need
transforming past problems

No desire to pick up again
destructive elements grasped
Now is time for release
Space for me to grow

Just give myself room
to be happy and free
No worries on this day
only recuperation

River flows on as I do
Being Grandma with Ella
such easy open smiles
uncomplicate my life

8 September 2007

Healing party
Jane's summer house
Murray's boat naming
going with daughter

Kerin reconnects
with Phung, Phuoc
breaking through past
just enjoy now

Lovely food
Bonfire sing
Warmth and light
Kerin so well

Oh, what grace
being with daughter
together with sangha
sharing good times

Thank you for this
special day/evening
Kerin, Sophie, Bob
my heart opening

Such healing
so grateful
Kerin loans her mum
Non-Violent Communication

20 September 2007

Coming to right time
Bob and I agree
Use ways and means
to clear rest of mortgage

Moment just feels right
Let go of grasping
Freed of mortgage payments
Expenses nearly break even

So method's come
for simple, easy living
Allowing Reiki practice
to grow just as it may

Giving me the space
to rest as well as plan
Grandchildren time
Releasing worry burden

I want to use dear Reiki
Please guide me to help heal
those around in need
that within which waits

SOPHIE SLEEPOVER

Childhood noises
Sophie, Kerin downstairs
pussycats, squeaks
reading, stories, songs

I wish you well
dear daughter of mine
I'm proud of you
finding own light

Meditating above
as church bells ring
Feeling brilliance
universe sparkle

SLEEPING OVER AT ELLA'S

Ella asleep
Nap time after lunch
Three days together
Bonding the more

Now she says words
I teach her 'it's stuck'
A useful phrase
for many occasions

In my arms
Racing ahead
Munching lunch
Becoming a child

In park she gathers sticks
to drop down bench holes
A city kid watching traffic
oblivious to background noise

Puppets and singing
Dancing with friend
Calling me 'Na na'
Touching my heart

13 October 2007

Retirement, funny thing
letting go, room to be
beyond worry schemes
into life's richness

From inner growth
comes next steps
Not pushing, giving space
for flowers to blossom

Seeing the grasping
for Childbirth Reiki
What I said I'd do
Something to prove

Liz asks, 'Prove to who?'
Friends feel the comfort
that I'm doing something
Open to nothing place

Roshasa on face
says take care of self
Release need to work
to just allow flow

Proving my worth
by getting paid
I want to help others
permit conditions to ripen

Reconciling with relation
such special progress
Allowing grace in
awaking without dread

Psychological reversal
of fear facing school
Laughter when can't read
return to Brooklyn sleep

Habit energy to worry
slip back into bad
May I reverse pole
so light can glow bright

Release from shoulders
Warmth of deep healing
Lifting the weight
so I may walk easy

Attainment is emptiness
Living process lets stream
meander where it may
Open to possibilities

Give time to recover
Explore new interests
without proof burden
Glad for family weekend

18 October 2007

INVITING THE BELL

Bell at eye height
Focus on rim
'sing' helps sound
beyond self conscious

Smiling at disharmony
also acceptable
Transformation, insight
special chance to process

Getting ego out of way
so energy flows natural
between bell resonance
and my true nature

I invite bell for ancestors
Buddhas and bodhisattvas
Sending heart with ring
vibrating with emptiness

Allowing sound to happen
Privilege to be medium
between Buddha and bell
Luscious being in that state

Family gathering
warm heart glow
Deep satisfaction
to see us connect

Resonating together
Harmonizing
Raising energy
of clan love

Each on own journey
rocky and smooth
Committed to each other
blossoming expands

Sophie and Ella
cousin connection
building between them
surrounded by our joy

Kvelling with *mazel*
Mazel tov to us all
Putting in the effort
hearts naturally open

Ancestors within
smile through our genes
increasing the power
of generations together

21 November 2007

Norwich to London
poetry readings
Grateful for Reiki
students and clients
Grandma connection
Sharing love with Bob

Fun in retirement
New life of work
Wondrous Reiki
giving to others
Poetry, advice
as OI sharing

Reading tomorrow
in heart of East End
of Jewish identity
where refugees landed
women transformed
as I do now

May I continue
moment by moment
to touch inner wonder
transform fear of jinx
Such beauty flows
in autumn streaked light

26 November 2007

Accepting blessings
naches, mazel
Life so vivid
down child slide

Black bird on bare tree
enjoys red berries
chirping vibrates
through her throat

I am so rich
when I allow
worry to stop
so joy can sing

New life a wonder
performing miracles
Reiki training
treatments transform

Poetry readings
beyond selling books
Sharing words
insights, *mishigas*

Ancestors' voice
authentic within
resounds through me
just as the bird

Reiki building
intuition
In that realm
I chirp for us all

New generations
coming up growth
Releasing apprehension
allowing them own way

Enjoying grandchildren
Their being a *mitzvah*
Rekindling my light
in beaut-e-ful ways

Mishpocheh
resonates
We laugh out loud
echoing each other

Mindful practice
Sangha meditation
Reciting precepts
with OI sisters

Such rich sounds
reverberating
Life's harmony
Accepting blessings

3 December 2007

Walking Med with Bob
across sun-streaked green
Solid energy together
as winter winds blow

Breathing in and out
in step synchronicity
As my mind slowly calms
the common changes form

Natural process
cow paddy on grass
soaking into earth
for landscape beauty

Little train sweet
Trees become 3-D
Our joint focus
supports us both

Perspective comes
I see more clearly
I can't control
only walk, smile

Wind blows through me
sweeping cares away
Allowing freshness
into my lungs

7 December 2007

Inner child
opening to love
Light, fluffy
warm holding

Dear little one
neglected no more
Now that we agree
I can care for you

When rejected
better not to need
If it's not coming
why even want?

Now that I'm truly
willing to give
we can cuddle
in soft, cosy place

Accepting affection
right there within
Allowing approval
At ease with self

Habits of old
dreading school
Morning confusion
of what can do right

I embrace you
dear weary darling
No need to run away
I'll hug you, my sweet

15 December 2007

In wakeful night
I dream of cellar
with sandy floor

In anger at Bob
I march up stairs
indented with tracks
of my earlier steps

Seeing I'm hurting myself
still I shout once more
Sandy tracks are clear
This pain is old habit

Oh, I can float instead
Yes, I can fly down stairs
wondrous feeling so light

Years since I used this power
up the other way and out
Recognised unfamiliar place

The marvel of floating
lightness of air movement
With sensation rekindled
I see tracks without fear
of blaming myself again

Trust this natural magic
Reiki to bring in flow
Free on breath cushion

19 December 2007

Inner heart
opening from back
slow release
of what I've seen

Old energy
seeking mistakes
fed on blame
building shame

I see you in me
and my daughter
Accepting myself
I accept her

Where am I going
I'm not sure
Just explore
Trust where taken

I breathe and breathe
into unknown
Kindness toward me
is the route map

There I journey
into past time
Patterns of old
darkness and fear

Why us?
Why blame Jews?
We take on your hate
into our hearts

I breathe in love
life support
This vision is hard
I see the fire

Fire light transform
into compassion
all that suffering
in burning York tower

I accept apology
of Christian minister
Allow my misgivings
Support consciousness

Ill at ease
yet also warm
Deep kindness
for all my mistakes

These are ground
on which I learn
when I don't let
guilt obscure

That negative energy
feeds on itself
To end suffering
I need to feed love

Understanding lights way
When I trust me to see
earnest inner wanderer
seeking unity of essence

In oneness I'm safe
a part of family
with challenges to grow
appreciate inner beauty

Touching that beauty
without being sucked in
to turmoil surround
Just the weather of life

41

7 February 2008

TET NEW YEAR BLESSING

Breathing is peace
Sitting happiness
Resonating
Concentrated

Beyond words
focused energy
Such relief
Joyful being

New Year blessing
of Phuoc, Phung
Vietnam
in my blood

Ancestors
mine, theirs
All together
in giant pool

So free
just relaxed
Breathing here
Touching keys

Awareness
faith worthy
Buddha within
lighting way

Birds rejoice
in my joining
back to oneness
energy moves

May I keep
without grasping
this sitting
expanding out

Thank you Thay
wondrous teacher
sharing wisdom
practice with us

May I share
mine with kindness
Thank you Mom, Dad
serenity, delight

Opening to dear Bob
returning SF partner
My cherished being
Understanding widens love

Coming back to self
with deeper insight
Leaves sway in wind
I reverberate

May my descendents
feel this goodness
contained within
opening to freedom

May all beings
in Year of Rat
feel the fun
of happy release

13 March 2008

White hot Reiki to Heart
deep in sleepless night
Fear of opening too far
wanting to go all the same

Oneness, no-self scary
releasing grasp control
Though clearly illusion
used to anchor my life

False anchor unsafe
Wonder of inner Buddha
brings deeper reality
I stand on edge to step in

I see this is insight not madness
yet having witnessed such decent
I fear loosing touch with reality
though this is real, true moment

Difference between mad delusion
and shining goodness within
no inner/outer distinction
is clarity of mind and solidity

Solid stability the core
of what seems like magic
Each step breathed on earth
slowly releasing false notion

Take your time
Nothing to seek
Allow insights
to naturally sink in

23 March 2008

Drive to Buddhist wedding
together breathing joy
Reading in Sangha ceremony
Happiness overflows

Matthew beaming smile
Anwen deep connection
Special relations with parents
Couple joins understanding

Dancing first waltz
Their union touching
Ceilidh fun follows
friends, relatives mingle

On long drive home
talk with Sangha pals
Charging patients difficult
Given childbirth contacts

Polish camaraderie
She tells of ideal
for structural change
I speak of inner growth

In dream, driving old van
turning into one way road
Traffic coming toward me
I safely back round

Navigation stress
seeing I can shift
Reversing direction
seeking new way

17 April 2008

*After spending three weeks in Lower Hamlet, Plum
Village Monastery and Retreat Centre, teaching English*

Return from magic Plum Village
of vivid purple, green Iris
A thousand stars in pre-dawn sky
Cloud walking on mother earth

Connecting with Sisters from Vietnam
laughing together at mouth contortions
needed for making English sounds
Touching hearts in joyous teaching

In meditation hall
stone temple with Sisters
focus of sangha energy
brings mind clarity

Earth touching release
to guilt habit depths
Naturally blaming self
from misguided loyalty

In clearness I find
true loyalty lies
in building self love
to shine out to others

When habit starts
realising true loyalty
helps to reverse
to loving cycle

Thay says keep good seeds
flowering long as can
Transform bad ones
as soon as possible

This lessens suffering
allows true career
of understanding
to blossom as Bodhisattva

20 April 2008

Double Birthday Wonder
after Plum Village opening
allowing my happiness
space to flower, grow

In glorious reversal
that guilt is disloyal
my wellbeing helps all
I befriend true self

Reunion enjoyment
Bob and I share
our hopes and fears
We come together

Kerin, Sophie birthdays
everyone right effort
Working in concert
with family warmth

Such improvement
Kerin has made
Developing herself
responsible for own life

Sophie school girl
Ella talking
Kev and Helena
building careers

I feel the power
from Lower Hamlet
of Sister's focus
Thay's deep wisdom

Taking his advice
positive seeds linger
Embracing negative
to return to store

Tired but content
Birds serenade
I rest and prepare
for Rahelly Passover

10 May 2008

Sister Jina white heart
Cream as we hug
In that special moment
receiving our connection
back thorough space/time

Transmitter
of fourteen trainings
Sisterhood shared
supporting ill women
without being caught

Living as part of Sangha
teaching Sisters English
Ease beyond resistance
flowing with the energy
Allowing me to be whole

Reconnection back home
with Sister Jina's hug
transmission so alive
touching inner happiness
Sister Jina and I are one

11 May 2008

After deciding to hold
40th 'anniversary' party
A chance to focus
on beauty of our love

Amidst justice struggle
demos, agit prop
we come together
budding affection

Through forty years
we blossom and grow
Working through problems
we journey together

All part of the adventure
we continue down stream
Insights enrich
the union of our love

*   *   *

Bloom of Sixty-eight
catalyst expanding
Consciousness shift
process continues

In life's renewal
generations explore
ways to peace, justice
Us part of movement

California Street romance
on Bob's foldout couch
A part of larger flow
world ripe for change

2 June 2008

Here in the garden of life
our love grows for forty years
branching to children, grandchildren
Allowing us to wander, explore

What precious time together
growing up, creating, connecting
Deepening through difficulties
Ripening through sun, storm

Within I discover true self
goodness of inner light
timeless one with all
Knowing that's what I am

Come on, stop pretending
It's too late for that now
Moment together too cherished
for fear and worry to distract

Such beauty in celebration
with family, friends surround
Warmth of deeply savouring
special fragrance of our love

Whatever the future brings
our energy bond continues
As garden mulch grows tomatoes
we enjoy new varieties

11 June 2008

After teaching the second level of Reiki, I practice what I've learned.

Reiki two lessons
here for me
teaching touches
symbols anew

Wonder of distant healing
Mental emotional balance
Re-triggered in my being
as I pass symbols to others

May power spin deep
into my self curing
Letting garden release
bring ease of growth

*   *   *

Grandpa Guilt
up from depths
White roots found
in ancestral soil

Asking Reiki
to heal the source
of guilt/self-blame
habit in me

Takes me to
place of pain
Dad's childhood
parent's anger

Their blame/guilt
for selves, each other
sets the pattern
for Dad's own fear

When I heal
my guilt/blame
I clear the way
Freedom for all

White roots tangled
in ancestor disputes
anger, fear, shame
Time for new start

I, their granddaughter
with own granddaughters
set wheel of healing
spinning for us all

May Reiki open way
for my renovation
light shining through
grandma, grandpa, beyond

Dear Grandma Esther
I feel our strong link
transforming your suffering
with my mindful steps

Holding hands
in walking med
with Esther and Harry
Conversion to love

Within me
through to them
our family reunites
in their future happiness

20 June 2008

Little Ella, wrapped up in bed
Us playing, like with my sister
Two little girls enjoying dolls
Singing our made-up song

Intimate, fresh miracle
reborn in new generation
Gentle surrender to just being
softly enclosed in timeless ease

Kev, Helena return, we all sing
Happy together in family affection
Each exploring in our own way
then coalescing, nurturing each other

30 June 2008

Richness of Sophie's desire
to learn to meditate like parents
In pebble breathing focus
Kerin, Sophie, I harmonise

May we peacefully practice
sweet energy flow
Anxiety coming to rest
settling into stillness

26 June 2008

After doing a series of Reiki Taster sessions in John Lewis' beauty treatment room

Tara insight
life force renewal
Bodhisattva
nurturing beings

John Lewis room
space of healing
when just outside
selling floor buzz

Compassion abounds
judgement held
in understanding arms
rocking base fear

Manager disappointed
more products not sold
I focus on treating women
They're amazed at release

Layers yet deeper
surfacing to release
way to freedom
of real aspiration

Great lesson for me
balancing business
with my true calling
of healing bodhisattva

Reiking nine women
fifteen minutes each
Given the chance
to live vocation

I trust to follow
deep way of love
will bring both harmony
and needed prosperity

Ordinary people
feeling within
peaceful vibrations
so different for them

1 July 2008

Fear of dying in sleep
Waking up just to check
still alive, in control
Afraid to succumb

Disturbed slumber
very old pattern
from past revisited
in hazy glimpse

Blue light through body
brings awareness relief
illuminating to essence
from whence I came

This fear habit is so deep
back to past manifestation
with torture there as well
Light can also shine through

Asking Reiki to heal
source of my night waking
brings up realization
in process of release

Releasing notions, concepts
of past lives, no separate self
gives contact with feeling
this link to understanding

Bird sings the answer
explaining beyond words
inner experience
warm summer of now

Surfacing to let go of
I don't know exactly what
Maybe it's not important
I just need to love the fear

I hold you in my arms
cradling darkness of past
in blue light of connection
healing way of this life

Bodhisattva aspiration
freedom to start with me
Clearing my channel
to glow out with ease

Rainbow bedroom light
succumbing to my own love
Warm Reiki life force
universal resonance

1 August 2008

Dream of enforcer me
Keep that woman in box
She is bad enemy
and I am in charge

Stop squirming in there
I expect you to be still
You annoy me
moving around

Suddenly my heart softens
Wait, she's a person
uncomfortable, stuck
I don't want to hurt anyone

Now she's a doll
blond with dress
in cardboard box
with plastic front

What a strange dream
Who is that doll?
Too blond to be me
but if not who else?

In Reiki treatment
I hear within
'Take that doll out
and play with her'

Meditating today
I do take her out
with a big hug
I hold her to heart

Yes, she's my doll
She and I are one
in holding her
the warmth spreads

14 August 2008

Dream of identity
all left behind
After no one breathing
a part of the whole

Not so scary
one with nature
Life is vivid
Cinematic

Sun reflected
upon the river
ripples pass
swans glide

Just walking
being each breath
Simply alive
beyond mind care

Needn't worry
dear friend ego
You are more
not any less

15 August 2008

Written to accompany photos I took for Visions of the City Magazine

CAMBRIDGE SUMMER

Meandering with River Cam
through summer afternoon
Shallow pond ripples
budding water lilies

On it's way to town
past common open greens
Cows there munch, stare
in cinematic scenes

Skirting shopping centre
posh new town arcade
Staying with simpler Cambridge
I'm on to Parker's Piece

Here in central square
Fair, music, French market
More like the old days
with community booths

Age COPE and schools
Humanists, Women's Centre
families, baby bulge
in city I call home

A foreigner I may be
but now I stand out less
on Mill Road just the norm
as culture mix enriches

Arjuna, health food co-op
Squatted social club
Small cafés with boards
where I post Reiki signs

Open Studio tradition
seeing art and homes
sharing throughout city
connection of our ways

Summer holiday shift
from Uni students to visitors
Foreign language learners
bike on wrong side of road

The edges now seem blurred
in town and gown divide
Market town, Microsoft
keeping city aboom

Then again in September
as the recession bites
with colleges still strong
will townies feel the nip?

18 August 2008

Do you know
you have Buddha Angels
my client asked
after deep treatment

No I answered
partly surprised
You didn't know
I'm a Buddhist

Their wings are white lace
emitting such light
They said they're Joy's
They're helping you

The powerful one
on my left shoulder
looked at you
with, oh, such love

Thank you angel energy
and chants I sing
My client hears
as church bells

Thank you to Reiki
and Buddha within
giving me confidence
for healing in and out

22 August 2008

Preparing to take Sophie on Thay's retreat

Opening to grace
strength to return
to my childhood flat
Shining mindful light

Giving attention
to second child
Recognition
I'm worthy, strong

Reconnecting
to true essence
There already
Familiar past smells

Five year old me
receiving extra care
Healing mixed message
Remembering parents' love

Preparing to take Sophie
five year old granddaughter
as my special charge
Such a great blessing

My dear Sophie
seeking calm
witnessing turmoil
valuing serenity

Mother Florence
who nurtured me
please be with us
transmit equanimity

Mom in my heart
tired but clear
in your descendents
your energy glows afresh

3 September 2008

A cell of all
All within
imprinted

Beyond clouds
of fear, doubt
Oneness shines

Releasing blame
for drifting away
White light appears

Vibrating in body
universe surround
resonates back

Just a part of the whole
No need to try, struggle
Merely being true self

Thay within smiles
as he did on stage
being interconnection

So at ease, loose
radiant happy
Lit up with love

4 September 2008

After Thay's Nottingham Retreat

*After taking Sophie
on retreat with Thay
Knowing her more
Growing closer*

Being with Sophie
within and without
Sharing my solidity
and her zest

Mom and Dad
in us both
helping us
open to life

Taken for granted
not getting angry
I offer Sophie
unconditional love

Giving myself
recognition I need
to accept Sophie
sparkling as she is

What's not wrong
Being with just that
Releasing expectations
we are both free

15 September 2008

Hooks coming out
Drama of loved-ones
back to childhood
swept into their need

From loving perspective
kindness to my fear
Seeing their pulling energy
destructive for us each

Compassionate detachment
yet again brings clarity
We are all the ones
dispersed in universe

In letting go of grasping
becoming part of whole
sharp hooks detach
float up to sun, melt

Looking down
from sky view
I can see progress
each time higher vision

Thank you for kindness
dear Sister Eleni
resonating within
New York Jewish warmth

Dear Mother, Thay
universe surround
in your deep healing
I smile to your love

Through this connection
Thay's light before stars
I come back to whiteness
transforming in new ways

In your wisdom
truth of essence
I feel the safety
to release, be one

Retreat growth
just keeps coming
Reiki synchronicity
Blessings galore

25 September 2008

Seen from higher level
up on spiral staircase
looking into past lessons
Kind to inner angst

I see ancestral fear
of Pogrom once again
Loosing all, forced on
into unknown blackness

What do they want from me
those ancestors who suffered so
'Ve just vant you should be happy
Don't you listen? Ve told you!'

To do that I must transform
the dark despair within
that I can't control
Save myself and others

Reversal yet again
as I walk by river
watching swans feed
seeing fear block

Spinning in wrong direction
fright closes my heart
Yet river ripples through
Insight vision reappears

I am not that important
just a speck of the whole
No superhuman powers
but inner shift reflects out

Loving depth of my fear
even if caught in worry
Being willow leaf sway
Roots feel the earth calm

29 September 2008

Looking down staircase
seeing how far I've come
Greater inner acceptance
loving the fear within

Needing to prove value
to male authority figures
and inner stern judge
that I'm worthy of love

Seeing those male authorities
have their own inside struggle
They too need understanding
I can accept us all

Letting go of notion
of male permission
from Buddha, Thay
within myself

May Reiki heal source
of my needy desire
for male approval
Fear of not making grade

Worried that not capable
of living up to standards
In future competition
always running behind

Loving scared little girl
afraid of boys' firecrackers
Seeking conditional love
to show I do count

Breathing here in present
from my true nature
exhaling misperception
letting go stale view

Safe in this now
instant of inhale
Oh, such freedom
Release brings smile

1 October 2008

I read this poem as part of a panel at the 40th Commemoration of the SF State University Strike for the first Ethnic Studies Department in the US

Back in 1967
this radical girl
came to San Francisco State
from Community Organising

Link with SDS project
for housing, rent strike
and Baltimore students
also on campus

So joining SDS
at SF State
seemed so natural
with other projects

Spring'68 blossoms
worldwide struggles
from France to SF sit in
for ethnic admissions

September revives
zest for justice
Me now living
with my SDS guy

In telescoped time
we now return
somehow grandparents
Still partners in love

Back then Black Student's Union
calls strike, sets demands
for department to study
hidden history, culture

Desire to define
their own destiny
In height of Black Power
BSU is leader

From the start
SDS backs strike
helps organise Committee
for White Strike Support

Now this may sound strange
but in emerging energy
for self determination
that was natural flow

Civil rights movement
exposed poverty, racism
clearly for all to see
desperate need for change

Police helped build strike
by beating BSU leaders
White students shocked
witnessing on campus
police treatment in ghettoes

More students joined strike
White Support Committee
As we picketed entrances
campus was polarised

Force field to do right
needed to make it happen
in our vision others students
part of solution or problem

SDS saw problem source
propping up racism
as Capitalist 'me first'
militarist system

At San Francisco State
more working class students
trained to keep system running
not to see bigger picture

From that larger vision
white students being used
To help them see how
we formed department caucuses

In Department of Psychology
students critiqued skewed view
that mental illness is within
divorced from socio-economic

When I gave MMPI test
to my SDS women friends
we came out actively antisocial
labelled 'juvenile delinquents'

We saw role of psychology
fitting 'deviants' back into system
So drink beer, watch TV burnings
of Vietnamese kids as Viet Cong

In Nazi Germany
was sanity beating Jews
and madness protesting
or other way round

For me as a Jew
connection was clear
with KKK Black hangings
and Nazi exterminations

White Student demands
for change in their courses
brought understanding
support for Ethnic Studies

As weather turned cold
and professors struck
'On Strike, Shut it down'
became a reality

Arrests at free speech platform
brought 450 down to jail
We women were processed
then put in large holding cell

Anyone seen as threat
like woman asking for milk
for girl with stomach ulcer
were put into solitary

From large holding cell
we began to hear screams
of scared young woman
picked off and confined

Alone in tiny cell
more frightening
than she could bear
she shouted to be free

When guards wouldn't listen
we acted together
banging and chanting
'Let her out', 'Let her out!'

Our call vibrated
throughout jail house
down to Bryant Street
supporter crowd below

In '69 Women's Lib sprouts
with some men still laughing
saying women's place prone
while others saw struggle link

Back in '67 at SDS Conference
woman asking us to meet
brought uproarious laughter
yet some women gathered

Problem with no name
begins to have words
Why are we left in background
Mostly not taken seriously

When women like me spoke at rallies
some guys just saw body parts
using long legs or large breasts
as excuse for eclipsing words

But in this time of rising
from Civil Rights to Ethnic Studies
struggling against oppression
helped us see ours as women

Earlier at Anti-Slavery Convention
barred for being female delegates
Mott and Stanton were inspired
to organise for women's rights

Strike women met when it ended
empowered by what we'd been through
Challenging old assumptions
exploring strengths, building movement

So the rebirth of feminism
was there in that holding cell
when, beyond fear, we chanted
'Let her out. Let her out!'

Guards dragged over fire hose
put nozzle through bars
Sudden force of water
knocking us off our feet

Drenched, we regained balance
and guards did let woman out
Our solid action together
resonating deeply

* * *

Forty years on lesson
power of energies united
Force beyond each one
belief in justice vision

Mass march together
Agit Prop Theatre
Running from police chase
hiding, swapping jackets

Scared facing jail unknown
but not wanting to disappoint self
be Germans just looking on at
packed cattle cars of human cargo

In that youth of belief
that we can change world
though seemingly impossible
shifts ripple through country

Now celebrate achievements
of College of Ethnic Studies
Women's Movement growth
Peaceful, prosperous Vietnam

Much writings of Strike, SDS
even England, Shoe Store School
Gordon DeMarco now passed on
Bob Biderman and I

I want to share lessons
of traps we fell into
perhaps could be useful
for generations now

Seeing in absolutes
that blinder limiting vision
to either all right or wrong
allows no way to come together

Sectarian in-fighting
finally destroyed SDS
Though reborn in this time
of new student challenges

It was our condemning vision
part of problem or solution
No middle ground possible
Needing to prove we're right

I used to work out of anger
feeling the force of its power
rush against social injustice
keeping me active in struggle

I just couldn't trust myself
to work from kinder emotion
For my external anger
also turned in on myself

Internalised as guilt
needing to prove I wasn't bad
seeing badness all round
limiting love getting through

Over decades life taught me
that anger is not most effective
Healing my own inner pain
compassion naturally flowed out

Better way to hand leaflets
against Iraq War
Not pushing them at 'others'
but handing each person peace

More people take leaflets
feel safer beyond judgement
to touch inner peace yearning
have common ground to speak

Listening, more important
than my talking to convince
in deeply hearing others
we find same core within

Then we see not separate
but interconnected
Poverty, racism hurts us all
in fairness we each benefit

5 November 2008   21 January 2009

OBAMA IS PRESIDENT

Back at SF State
in Sci Fi mode
Forty years later
Black President

'On strike, shut it down!'
to 'Obama, Obama!'
Interracial hugs
Re-blooming hope

Just possibilities
as Obama said
Make him do it
as Belafonte told

But somehow fitting
to be back on quad
New generation emerges
again to save the world

Waking up to Obama
as new President
Warm sun shinning
clear through cold

Amazing symbol
of America at best
Patchwork of cultures
sewn into one blanket

Two million brave freeze
World watches on
enjoying shift
Spirit of hope

In our lifetime
seeming impossible
African-American
wins majority

Best candidate
way beyond colour
In desperate times
we send him blessing

18 November 2008

Walking on green
with my love
though thousands
of miles away

Sun breaks through clouds
warming blue sky
reflected on river
swan gliding through

Accepting what is
Me, here with leaves
You, there helping
your dear mother

Beauty/pain at once
presence of both
Vivid light, dark shadow
life essence through all

Fluffy clouds sail
across clear sky
The kind Fannie likes
artistic, not boring

11 December 2008

Clear blue sky
sun shines through
cold crisp air
Bob's coming home
Life is wonderful

River ripples on
I slowly walk
feeling solid earth
releasing future plans
How would I know what's best?

Life twists and turns
just as Cam flows
I enjoy the sun
shining on my face
Now the only time

17 January 2009

BREATHING FOR GAZA

Gaza children cry
bleeding in terror
Young generation
makes victory sign

Fear, anger, revenge
of Israeli, Palestinian
feeding their deaths
haunting their lives

The Jew within
feels Israeli guilt
As Buddhist breaths
glimpsing peace

So many Gaza children
caught in line of fire
I am so very sorry
to see you suffer

Israelis, too, suffering
trapped in death cycles
Holocaust nightmare
never again victims

Hamas also
playing out fear
Palestinian families
so long held down

Shame or pride
oppressed or oppressor
Dualistic notions
to be released

Breathing in calm
Breathing out fright
Clarity is there
in every breath

Struggling to convert
inner heaviness
to openly spread
love's sheer light

At CamPeace demo
holding my sign
'Peace is Possible
the UN way'

Freeing from storm
back to deep roots
Feet touching earth
outside Guildhall

Breathing in warmth
breathing out peace
into collective energy
of clarity accord

May peace come
to Holy Land
So its peoples
may see they are one

*   *   *

20 January 2009

Intimate breathing
more vivid with self
Instant by instant
inner life clears

After listening to Thay
on sleepless night
Suddenly noticing
how I keep myself awake

Mara comes
as tense dread
of agonising
night ahead

What a flash
seeing mindset
Wave through body
of stiffening worry

Childhood habit
fearing dreams
soon became
sleepless ache

Feeding Mara
feeding fear
with body tension
Circular pattern

Trusting Thay
Feeling within
Being breath
I can enjoy

Revelation
once again
No problem
in this instant

Allowing my body
to release tension
No need to punish
for finding weakness

Receiving Reiki
rediscovering
watching supports
beyond judge

Embracing dear Joy
accepting you as is
beyond harsh view
lies inner goodness

That special knowing
smile before birth
Holding that close
opening my heart

23 January 2009

There in my name
Mom's deep wish
That I am joy
for me and all beings

This is my mission
Mom gave for this life
only in relaxed faith
can I allow it to happen

Reconnecting with Mom
beyond judging us harshly
Her insight returns
self growth to help world

Earlier image
of spider plant babies
I continue for you
You are within me

As you pass away
sleeping near Mom
You bestow
great gift upon me

Right after your death
I cry, you pet my hair
Now allowing myself
to receive your tender love

Being with Mom
in our connection
I breathe for you
We breathe together

In cherished photo
you smile back at me
In every cell of my body
you smile within

I release trying
again and again
to let inner joy
naturally shine

Nothing to prove
attain, achieve
in just being
life breathes through

1 February 2009

Staying at UK Interbeing Sangha's newly acquired first practice centre

Being with sangha
at new practice centre
Honoured to be
among first to sleep
under her roof

In circle of sharing
of faith's true meanings
reflected through us
energy vibrating
in mindful growth

Feeling Thay's presence
Walking pebbled path
tread by Sister Annabel
Plum Village comes
to Dorset, UK

2 February 2009

Once back from Being Peace Cottage after Dharma Training Retreat

Snow meanders in white slivers
covering earth in her softness
Piling high upon the land
Giving grandchildren
first real snowy day

Child within smiles, laughs
heart opens to memories sweet
re-enacted in white crunch step
Now I am light, free to enjoy
wondrous waves of snow upon us

13 February 2009

Kerin Miracle
done herself
her Buddha Nature
shining clarity

Thank you Buddhas
Bodhisattvas
Kerin's Sangha
Her desire to grow

As I see, change
within my true self
respecting, accepting
my special daughter

Feeling interconnection
compassionate detachment
Kerin nurtures my faith
in each of our practice

May we continue to heal
Dharma light upon us
loving ourselves
shining out to us all

17 February 2009

27 February 2009

Sophie here
special week
delivering her
to kid's play group

Being with Ella
so uncomplicated
alone together
laughing, playing

I tell her my job
most important
enjoying life
in the moment

Tired, happy
confident within
Mom there too
to share with us

She's surprised
smiles wide
easily accepts
happy in herself

Ella expressive
saying loves me
Hugging farewell
Kev, Helena warmth

So self possessed
this little girl
expecting love
in family surround

Easy within
taking in stride
flexible to relish
life as it comes

She likes all colours
makes cards for us all
happy to stay with us
and go to play group

So much to learn
from little Sophie
Staying in now
freedom to savour

28 February 2009

**After reciting the 14 Mindfulness Trainings with
British Order of Interbeing members in the UK
and Japan, via SKYPE, with some technical
difficulties**

Across continents
we managed to meet
Reading trainings
we hold so dear

Touching hearts
through interruptions
Breathing patience
to reconnections

Like old fashioned
communication
in fussy feedback
commitment shone

31 March 2009

Releasing dark double back anew
Old pattern of negative whip
just as I'm feeling relaxed
shutting down heart opening

There I see you old habit
appearing as thoughts, fears
Anger sucking mindfulness away
I watch, accept who you are

Your power of taking over
comes from my not noticing
I need kindness for my pain
seeing through to your essence

Warmth, protection, love
vigilance for judge of bad
Not giving grasping the power
but smiling to old pattern again

Allowing Reiki light through
Spring budding bare branches
touching big me within
watching, allowing cloud to pass

Seeing other's fear within
judgment raising as guilt
Anger brings wave of angst
rekindling old mind pattern

Breathing into all of nature
allowing anger, fear to release
Trusting wonder of life
Beauty of Bob's SF return

20 April 2009

DAY OF MINDFULNESS

Returning anew
fresh spring start
Vivid beauty
birdsong vibration

On this clean page
turned from troubles
lush green expanse
deep purple tulips

Speaking with sangha
of my difficult time
echoing within
fear, tangled mind

Outside all day
in splendour of fields
sharing mindfulness
life's challenges

Witnessing our growth
faith in our practice
Supporting awareness
of the wonders of being

Nature blossoming
yellow, pink, green
Heart widening
Returning anew

26 April 2009

4 May 2009

Savouring family
weekly gathering
Sophie, Kerin
Bob and I

Eating, cooking
planting, playing
listening, talking
Keeping up to date

Kerin, Sophie
part of our lives
sleeping here
every Friday night

Tasting sweetness
and difficulty
Helping each other
be constructive

Together this weekend
Accepting one another
Loving us all
Savouring family

Touching safe place
Being in un-birthday
Childhood home calm
playing dolls with Susan
Mom's surrounding love

Teaching un-birthday
to Ella so cosy
Comfy, warm playing
Time is gone
Tree blossoms flower

Mothering returns
Dancing together
Kerin, Sophie, Ella
Kev, Bob and I
Enjoying family

8 May 2009

MY MAGIC LIFE

Joy lives by the common
overlooking the river
White blossoms fill tree
as dharma rain falls

Her life partner, Bob
shares her space, being
They love one another
grow, support each other

Children, Grandchildren
come to them and stay
bringing young energy
challenges and sweetness

She meditates, writes
and teaches Reiki
Treating people
when they appear

Difficulties come and go
passing like the clouds
Awakening seeds within
touching fear and sorrow

Surrounding seeds with love
they take time to recede
strengthening Joy's focus
feeding Beginner's Mind

Reiki share with Liz
washing away tension
allowing cleansing energy
to shine on magic life

11 May 2009

Seeing dandelion root
deep inside my belly
Worry generations long
culture of always problem

Even when times are good
the root sends up shoots
Perhaps I take it too seriously
I just need to say 'worry'

I feed it power with fear
annoyance that you stalk me
When it's merely a joke
an old Jewish hobby

Laughing, I embrace life
our culture so much more
Big warm bear-hugs
Family celebrations

Dandelion flowers are lovely
and their leaves make soup
Covering the ground with joy
allows transformation at base

12 May 2009

Helena funded for PhD
We're so proud of her
Embracing Irish women
with empowerment anew

Fresh life chapter
giving Helena, Kev
more financial security
for creative pursuits

Though future unknown
this hardworking couple
get special chance
to explore their muse

24 June 2009

After attending the Path of the Buddha Retreat in Plum Village

Twenty one days
with Thay and Sangha
Breathing as one body
Collective consciousness

Releasing, transforming
hearing for first time
Thay's clear message
This is object of my mind

Subject and object
manifest together
Suddenly I see
my judgement overlays

When I release them
life is clear ease
Just instant by instant
consciousness reborn

Working together
meeting Responsaholic
What a relief
to just let her go

Sangha family bonding
sharing about Mom
Beyond critical pattern
touching her purity

Remembering
our true link
her deep love for me
Feeling us reconnect

Strength of Sangha Mind
healing of hamlet earth
Power of process
Thay's wisdom, energy

May these changes
insights, healing
deeply root within
Reborn hearing bell

Listening, really listening
exposing every cell
to curative vibration
Open to Bodhisattva

12 July 2009

Publicising Bat Nha
Compassion for all
Nurtured in chanting
brings connection
with clearer energy

Avalokiteshvara
for Bat Nha temple
loving kindness
understanding

Loosening knots
of misperception
allowing compassion
to penetrate deep

In myself
seeing knots
loosening allows
heart focus

Loving kindness
flowing through
as I let go
more clarity for Bat Nha

May balm of kindness
cover all involved
May nuns and monks
be safe, clear, fed

20 July 2009

ONENESS

Bringing together
my spiritual practices
Zen, Reiki, Chi Kung
Allows me to be whole

Open freedom
in the moment
Usui San Buddhist
Thay within, smile

Body and mind
in perfect oneness
Energy flow
in earthed position

Reiki teaching
integration
Buddhist reality
Chi energy

24 July 2009

BECOMING THE REIKI MASTER YOU ALREADY ARE

Written as part of my Reiki 3A Master Practitioner Course Manual

More than an attunement
Reiki Master Practitioner
you can only become
through your own efforts

Wondrous process
beyond worry
opening to being
energy each moment

Harmonising within
focused through meditation
allowed to mature
by living as Reiki Master

Moment by moment
mindful way of life
Resonating Reiki
within and without

Yes, you can do it
your sun shining through
generations of clouds
heavy fear, doubt

Stepping in footsteps
of Usui Sensei
energy of teacher
there for us to be

So it's worth vow
(no connection to sin)
to make effort each day
to practice Reiki in life

19 August 2009

DREAMING OF DAD

Swimming in sea with Dad
So nice to see him again
We go deep under water
Surprise, I'm not drifting back up

Sudden fear I might drown
Intensity so profound
Need to let grasping go
Truly trust I'm safe

As I do I drift up
Energy pulling toward light
Letting air slowly out
even before I surface

Breaking through water
freshness fills lungs
Pleasure of being alive
Enjoy in-breath with Dad

30 August 2009

After going on retreat with Sophie

Sister Annabel
permeating through us
at Family Friendly
UK Retreat

Manifesting
with each breath
our collective effort
making it happen

Pitching-in together
with children, food
washing, setting up
inviting the bell

Fresh kid energy
holding our hands
joyfully playing
silently eating

Through rain, sun
with wide vistas
across chequered fields
at Being Peace Centre

Sangha energy
growing clearer
Transformations
Summer expansion

Understanding, Compassion
Two Promises Ceremony
Granddaughter receives name
Precious Forest of the Heart

7 September 2009

Satisfied this instant
with my life
Satisfied with self
that's a bit harder

Don't listen to her
ancient voice persists
Jewish guilt, judgement
surrounds all, can't win

Means of control
fear of God power
Vulnerability of life
always on guard

More than a joke
when on his birthday
Dad said with a smile
'Mine enemy grows older'

My dear father within
I dare to transform
for us and ancestors
that enemy with love

Satisfied with self
seems a contradiction
as vow to improve
but look how far I've come

Acknowledging deepening
higher self awakening
Satisfied with Joy, Dad
in this very instant

From this perfection
opening to compassion
I walk gracefully in light
embracing mistakes

10 September 2009

Written for my revised Reiki Level 1 manual

What is Reiki
this nurturing energy
spiritually guided
washing out obstructions

I feel it through me
tingling waves
Energy vibrations
cleansing old habits

Seeds remain
generations old
Picking weed shoots
Transforming compost

Intending compassion
Watching fear distraction
Just for today, now
do not worry, anger

Life practice
Awareness growing
River flowing timeless
All interconnected

No distinction
Reiki within/without
Opening to abundance
allowing healing through

Trusting process
Being Reiki flow
Ripples spreading
spiritual energy

30 September 2009

After sadness, fear
Violence on monastics
routed from Bat Nha

Difficulties surround
Instability abounds
Anger used as device

Return to inner island
where life stream flows
Beauty of safe focus
washing through negative

Birdsong sends shivers
beyond binds of mind
obsession with drama
sadness at Bat Nha

In refuge of Buddha
mindfulness within
energy shines through me
glowing out in all directions

Conscious breathing
brings protection
for body and mind
returning as one

Skandhas reuniting
layers interweaving
to be my true self
Return to inner island

4 October 2009

***After meditating for Monks and Nuns
from Bat Nha***

Breathing as Sangha body
we meditate together
Here in Cambridge
There in Bao Loc

Chanting to Avalokita
vibration so strong
Healing energy
for all those involved

White heart petals
blowing in open
Spiritual ancestors
sit with sangha

May harmony pervade
sweet honey spreading
Healing deep wounds
Nurturing us all

16 October 2009

Amsterdam return
Trip went so well
Bob and I reunite
on ground of Adventure

Old motorcycle trip
so many years ago
Camping and cooking
staying so long

Culmination
of our road trip
in such good spirits
Amsterdam received us

We wanted to stay
but housing shortage
and me, pregnant
with spinach mad monkey

Whatever happened
all part of Adventure
We return again now
to our sweet romance

Ready for the break
weathering our lives
So many tears, smiles
we've grown from together

Amsterdam's grown too
Bright coloured spirit
to create and change
Remains dynamic

Enjoying together
finding us funny
Affection so deep
Respecting each other

With eyes clear
to beauty of city
our inner beauty
appreciating anew

Romancing Amsterdam
Remembering past lives
together in this city
we shed our worries

Rippling canals
sun shining through
reminding each other
of sweetness of life

21 October 2009   29 October 2009

CHILDBIRTH AWAKENING

Awakened in the night
Dear neighbour in labour
Contractions so close
barely giving a break
Mother breathes wise
knows to change positions

Rushes so strong
birth force intense
Reiki comes through
not attached to results
Holding her hand
praising her work
Baby soon born
on reaching hospital

Birth experience
Meeting challenge
Helping to grow
Safely ride waves

My fascination
intensity time
Body transforms
to open to life

Reiki, breathing
our support
Mum's awareness
key to success

With trusting focus
She is empowered
Body dance with baby
Being part of whole

27 October 2009

Wall to wall offspring
blessings, hard work
Kev sleeps in my study
his energy so good

Kevin's sweet being
creative, responsible
Kid play, our sharing
widening my heart

Sophie and Ella
connecting together
next generation's
warmth of glow

Kerin unique
making own way
Trying NVC
discussion on me

Beyond difficulties
staying in present
Sophie eager, happy
says Ella, Kev gift

Such strong bond
Sophie and Kerin
Good for each other
laughing and singing

After four days
Bob, I breathe quiet
Smile to family
enriching our lives

2 November 2009

Different perspectives
as I walk round
sculpture called 'Joy'

Spiritual teachers
back to Buddha
Mindful breathing

Earth Goddess
Reiki life force
Nature's growth

Parents, ancestors,
descendents transmit
energy I can use

Form of this body
Woman, mother
flesh and Chi

Feelings so mixed
love and disgust
for this being

Sense perceptions
looking through lenses
of past experience

Mental formations
arising, descending
Objects of mind

Store Consciousness
deposit of seeds
with this person

So what does it look like
this sculpture called 'Joy'?
Perspective comes and goes

Wide as universe
narrow as misperceptions
I wipe glass clearer

Better to see
just this now
Autumn beauty

Don't avoid question
Ache in gut
just minor distraction

From wider view
I see your goodness
connection to all

Energy tingles
as I sit breathing
smiling to 'Joy'

Laughing
So serious
this dear creature

I support you
'Joy' is this moment
to live and grow

3 November 2009   30 November 2009

REIKI SHARES

Liz and Rahelly   Rahelly and Liz
each holding one side   hold my shoulders
In their hands   giving me Reiki
heat melts to softness
                               Feeling needy
We have something special   Sorry for myself
three friends together   Why happening to me?
Sharing life's challenges
Spiritually guided   Through Reiki I hear,
                               'It's perfect.
As we disperse   Your getting just
following own path   the challenges you need.'
We are still there
holding each other   'Ok then,' I accept
                               taking Reiki into
                               my deep cavern
                               Allowing it to fill

                               'Stay in the present.
                               Your worries are
                               about the future.'

                               Then I remember
                               the future won't be
                               the way I expect

19 November 2009

At Phuoc, Phung Temple
facilitating last night
Kerin, Murray there
I focus concentration

Guided meditation
for the new people
Spiritual ancestors
power coming through

Beyond worry, fear
I am steady flow
A part of Sangha Mind
energy so clear

One with whole
alignment lucidity
I find support within
balanced stability

Feeling bell vibration
Mind Temple harmony
Spreading through body
rippling out peace

21 November 2009

Reciting 14 Trainings
together via SKYPE
Sharing our intention
to live Bodhicitta

Taking turns reading
Feeling healing deep
Seeing my actions
during past month

Yes, I see the growth
and the mishaps too
Ways I'd like to change
beyond the block of guilt

Breathing with the bell
Trainings light the way
of how I want to go
No need to attain

Feeling the currents
of my inner stream
spiritual ancestors
joining us as well

Our mindful force
sustains through obstacles
Sharing our direction
brings more power to it

24 November 2009

Susan connect
healing deep
understanding
our need to be 'good'

Raised with guilt
as a control
I did the same
with my own kids

Later insight
aided my change
Now feeling harmony
is further release

Our Dear Mom
You meant so well
Later you grew
gaining serenity

Susan and I
each of your hands
So different and yet
part of your whole

29 November 2009

Inner island return
after challenging days
Three with problems
forcing me to grow

Meditation, Breathing
Reiki, patient practice
Doing best I can
No need to be perfect

Two birds atop
bare autumn tree
rising to sky
grey but still light

Clarity, insight
from safe island
Can not control
nor save others

Smiling to
fear distraction
Healing self
is all I can do

From that place
true compassion rekindled
Not drawing out my energy
but shining from full light

What is touched
seeing others' distress
is my own hurt
asking to be healed

With perspective
compassionate detachment
Awareness glows
out to those in need

15 December 2009

Sun beaming way
through worry cloud
Mara delusion
other's power over me

Seeing, embracing
fear pattern repeated
as if bully energy
has force of its own

Taking in light
heart widens
resonating with monks, nuns
practicing though harassed

Inspired by Bat Nha monastics
Bao Loc Abbot protecting
Angry crowd can't sway him
They are but object of mind

Breathing, clearing
Morning brightness
Freshness to depths
Feeling my energy

From this place
of fullness surround
Birdsong beauty
Happiness moment

Mara still comes
I see you passing
Your power diminished
with broadening awareness

21 December 2009

CAMBRIDGE SANGHA
WINTER RETREAT

Arriving through snow ground
Sangha Mind's calm embrace
Shift to deeper level
Surprised how much I'm holding

Yellow sun whitens
virgin fields surround
Mind eases in sharing
being cell of whole

Unspoiled snow shines
bright in all directions
Bare tree branches spread
widening awareness

Breathing as one
Consciousness collective
Meditation circle
Working together

Laughing, sharing
lightening hearts
Winter's bright sun
at the solstice

13 January 2010

TREE ART

What a work of art
you are dear tree
Out my bedroom window
dancing in fading light
Bare branches expose your core

14 January 2010

Birds perch atop
swaying branches
without fear

Calm view
against grey sky
Twittering heard

103

22 January 2010

Same nature
as great beings
My true nature
is the fabric

Interwoven
no location
Here with me
there with them

Loose weave
Great textile
Blanketing me
our true being

Receiving benefit
of their power
Embracing heart
bone of fear

Breathing through
softening centre
Concentration
warming chest

Smiling as I heal
compassion arises
If I want great beings
they are here with me

Heart widening
exhaling pain
Such sadness
to be supported

Propelled deeper
by difficulty
Thay says when still
simple solution

Resolution
not by other's grace
Mindfulness shows
way out from within

Teacher Lieu Quan
eyes burn through time
Penetrates to me
receiving energy

Disciple of
ninth generation
reads your poem
glimpsing insight

Connecting with
happy little girl
freedom to enjoy
still so alive

Hearing birdsong
resonating within
Beauty of
same nature

9 March 2010

Beautiful possibilities
for present and future
Opening to the light
healing now helps later

Closed defensive
only brings negative
Other's suspicions
I don't need to catch

Staying in wider view
vibrating with universal
Seeing planning mind
Smiling with compassion

From there not drawn
into other's dark tangles
Shifting to Thay's vision
going back to island ease

Legal arrangements
framework for peace
Intelligent Compassion
supports us all

So many good things
also happened yesterday
Kev's MA form in
nice talk with course leader

Bob and I booked
flat in fishing village
My flight, his return
Him planning train trip

Allowing all this positive
to embrace my heart, mind
From this place of beauty
I tingle with life's energy

The future made up
of all these moments
New directions for me
Beautiful Possibilities

29 March 2010

SANGHA FRUITS

Power of Sangha Mind
meditating with nuns
Cambridge group vibration
stronger than sum of parts
Energy beyond egos

Immersed in sweet wholeness
thoughts, fears still come, go
Yet held in Sangha embrace
I return to before-birth smile
Enjoying, I like to linger

Walking Med with friends
feeling our focused movement
Stepping into prior footprints
multiplies our own awareness
Seeing others reminds
reinforces earthed flow

In Hugging Med touching hearts
Connection with each person
brings about a special sharing
nurturing, protection, warmth

In Sangha food productions
what colours, taste potential
Satisfaction in mouth eating
silently savouring together

Watching sisters, brothers
reinforces return to self
Allowing passing distractions
back to yummy tongue
Held in collective focus

So helped by Listening, Speaking
learning from other's struggles
Still remember said of loft building
much easier when not worrying

That closeness in silent circle
open space to hear or share
can help build my courage
to tell deep heart sadness

Knowing from past experience
sangha listening concentration
will help put in proportion
present difficulty in my life
Drawing back the camera lens
to once again see bigger picture

Supported by OI Sangha
our collective deep desire
to live the fourteen trainings
best we can though imperfect

So grateful to practice with you
on SKYPE and in person
to nurture our commitment
Opening to now happiness

11 April 2010

Find the best
reversal of worst
Heart muscle practice
Smile, open wide

Plans pass
fear embraced
Lesson clear
be affirmative

Brain wired
so positive helps
Reinforcing fear
collects worry neurons

Shock of seeing
from open heart
my wishes granted
not as expected

Sophie asks Kerin
to come with us
on Thay's retreat
Kerin agrees

Best for them each
and them together
Yesterday positive
I open to energy

Don't know what
future will bring
But worry obstacle
brings distraction

Releasing control
allowing love blossom
Unique flower
appears in own way

12 April 2010

Touching earth
pouring out heart
back to first Mum
great transformer

Releasing attachment
to difficult people
Wishing them well
but clearly destructive

Letting go to nurture
pink soft awareness
Wrapping in protection
where light can get through

Opening window
allowing in sun
Spring has come
I grow anew

15 April 2010

Sharp edged white walls
right here in my mind
No need to worry
they hold up no ceiling

Vast sky above
when I see beyond
own limited vision
to sunlight healing

Water flows below
Walls just illusion
Life steams on
back to the sea

Glad I noticed walls
of 'should be my way'
just as I built them
expectations planned

Laughing and laughing
what joke construction
All I need do
is release my grip

Safer to flow with energy
changing ever recycling
Back to source of love
where no need for walls

Meeting Bob in Corfu after his European travels

Cool balcony shade
on warm afternoon
Birdsong full
Neighbours pass

Lovely last night
Yes, so sincere
Corfuites host
heart-warming drinks

Village opening to us
embraced in their magic
Olive tree gardening
fresh herbs, lemons

Vivid smells
crisp, intense
Koola and Christus
Show us their way

English neighbours
so much a part
In welcoming spirit
language blurs

Sun freshens sight
lighting up green
of ferny patches
below olive trees

White stone path
Wild flowers galore
yellow and purple
shining in the sun

Water blue, turquoise
me finally immersed
Home at last
a fishy can breathe

Stuffed vine leaves
and spinach pie
Taste treats with Bob
after tingling cool swim

17 May 2010

Bird in house lesson
Omen to bring clarity
It flew into glass
trying to get out

Bird's own force
shocked it back
As I opened door
it moved over to pane

Poor thing in a panic
at only place no exit
Going back into obstacle
surely injuring itself

Could it still fly?
Did it come in as hurt?
Trying to help bird
pacing behind glass

Fright had restricted
sense of wider view
Bird kept flying into pane
resisting assistance

All round was freedom
open window, door
Yet bird hurt itself
seeing just one way out

I tried lifting it to window
It wouldn't go that high
Kerin picked up bird
but it only got away

Bob said keep it low
take across to the door
As I managed to coax it
I hoped it could still fly

Off it went, Wings Wide
back out to the garden
Fear had trapped bird
But it was free all along

11 June 2010

I spent ten transformative days with Thay, Monastics and Lay Sangha at the European Institute of Applied Buddhism, attending the first OI Europe Retreat

OI Europe Retreat
Thay tells of Tiep Hien
True meaning of words
to deepen our practice

Tiep means to receive
accept the transmission
from spiritual ancestors
Watch Thay, others practice

Tiep means to continue
this wonderful tradition
Back from Ly, Tran Dynasties
Buddhism Engaged

Tiep means to be in touch
with life around, within
Growing, enjoying
Learning from suffering

Hien means Now
Sense contact perceived
This sound, colour paradise
Present Reality

Hien means to realise
Break free from net trap
Practice to freedom
of what's really here

Hien's Manifestation
appropriate now
Updating to suitable
actualisation

Tiep Hien meaning
is Order basis
Buddhism in the World
applied to daily life

Spiritual practice
energy makes strong
Teaching through example
We practice for us, others

OI lay members
stretch arms out into world
To be with other's suffering
we must touch, heal our own

Thay fires our hearts
not to waste life
Inspiring volition
to breathe, step to freedom

Receiving the Now
Continuing Realisation
Accepting Manifestation
ever changing

13 June 2010

After Thay's German Day of
Mindfulness at EIAB

In German Translation
of Thay's loving speech
I come home to my Yiddish
that I have so missed

Beloved mother tongue
so rarely spoken
lives on for me now
in its German root

A Jew at home with Thay
in Waldbrol transforming
Understanding, forgiving
We all grow together

I joyfully sing
Jewish song of peace
in old Nazi building
becoming spiritual centre

This mindful power
I touch on earth
With heart opening
I walk with German Sangha

15 June 2010

At the retreat, I ended up sleeping in the large, original multi-story EIAB building – which has had various uses reflecting German history.

House of Transformation
I've been drawn to you
A Jew in Nazi building
Mother in Maternity Ward

But you are so much more
And, of course, so am I
Beyond dualistic concepts
we are life ever changing

I don't want to be caught
but to grow beyond my limits
Allowing unconditional love
to wash away the pain

Thay sleeps in same building
Sister Annabel and Jina too
And so I sleep there well
Supported by the Sangha

House of Transformation
for post-cold war soldiers
Easing my inner war
I've softened being here

Dream of building ancestors
compassion for human pain
both physical and mental
can heal in place of love

Even the 'Aryan' vision
imposed in anger here
could not resonate its hate
but be war veterans refuge

Flowers blossom anew this spring
I smile a part of their bloom
In mother nature's nurturing
Restoring Life of the Heart

26 June 2010

Our son Kevin
staying over
Confident, clear
energy still sweet

Busy life
Father, Teacher
Photographer
Creative person

His positive attitude
makes the difference
Flowing with what comes
Being with what happens

Sitting once again
in living room
talking together
Now all adults

Him ironing shirt
Telling Ella story
Preparing to take
wedding photos

Working out
MA part time
Family man
Now in his 30s

5 July 2010

Witnessing Bob and Olivier
Their friendship so very deep
Precious for them both
sharing their lives together

Thirty-five year connection
from fathers to grandfathers
Thinkers, writers, warm-hearted men
Transformation and growth

Synchronicity of their meetings
keeping in touch across waters
Each exploring their journey
then reporting back, reflecting

Blossoming in own ways
Male energy of sweet flowers
Unique, creative, authentic
Supportive bond intertwines

7 July 2010

SAVOURING OUR
CREATIVE NOW

Three days of being with friends
sharing their energies with Bob
Us being each other's memory
Free flow experience exchange

Laughing with my best pal
hugging, sharing meals
each of us 'but I'm just...'
Laughing once again

Our gentle intertwine
consciousness collective
Living muse vibration
supporting creativity

Romance of life reborn
Magic of precious surround
This heaven time together
resonating our dreams now

Process all there is
Sweet writing practice
Future is built of this
instant we savour together

12 July 2010

Wiping off the mirror
to see myself more clearly
Truly look me in the eye
Smile at who smiles back

Releasing gut grip
from dark forest
of what is my power
long neglected

Under layers
of dead leaves
mulch so rich
it illuminates

Presence so soft
healing and gentle
shines right through
when I let ego go

True me so thrilling
tingly ease Vibe
Non-effort release
Better for all beings

Adding to collective
peace consciousness
Smiling at my dear
ego dysfunction

Distancing from
limiting thoughts
Seeing true nature
I'm so much more

Allowing process
Slow healing
Not same person
I was before

No going back
that Joy's not here
Embracing me all
with Ultimate delight

16 July 2010

I wrote these poems to be included with Five Mindfulness Training Certificates for those who would take the trainings with Thay in Nottingham.

RECITING FIVE MINDFULNESS TRAININGS

Wondrous step
on awakening path
Five Mindful Trainings
guide toward light

Sangha support
so very helpful
We do it together
Walking in peace

Reciting five trainings
together so strong
We want to invite you
to practice with us

At Mindfulness Days
in many Sanghas
Five Mindful Trainings
recitation practice

If not yet connected
to a local Sangha
see our website
to help you find it

If you can't get out
to go to a group
there's Deep Listening
Telephone Sangha

To recite the Five Trainings
if you can't get to Sangha
we're starting teleconference
recitation group

Why not set date
once a month with self
to feed your true nature
by reciting the trainings

STAIR MEDITATION

Bringing mindfulness
into daily life
Our usual steps
can lead the way

Stairs in our home
at work or on route
We can agree
to link with breath

Thay sets us reminders
to build our practice
So good to use contact
between breath and step

In, in, Out, out
Personal contract
with daily use stairs
becomes a habit

No need to be perfect
No judgement involved
Just come back with a smile
Conscious breath, step bond

So why not try it
Build into your life
precious reminders
of beauty right now

20 August 2010

27 August 2010

Written after Thay's retreat, which I went on with Kerin and Sophie.

Thay's radiance contagious
Loosening narrow hold
My heart opens wide
Accepting, one with sangha

Six days together
such transformation
Mind clearing vision
supports our family

In Sister Jina shawl
Wrapped in resonation
Such peace breathing
Happiness sitting now

My dear teacher
Tiep Hien transmitter
Hugging connection
Skilful smiling glow

No separate Joy
Such great ease
Afflictions light
clearly illusions

Old separation fear
Mom, Dad gone
dissolves as I feel
them in my blood

In being big me
heart centre opens
to yet another level
Just breathing, sitting

Responsible worries
Guilt misplaced
Nowhere to feed
when habit me not there

Covering Sister Jina
with my shawl when cold
has brought it back to me
with such special resonance

8 September 2010

I was still reaping the benefits of going with my daughter and granddaughter to Thay's retreat. Sometimes we did pebble meditation together and one morning I thought I'd try it by myself. This poem grew out of my sit.

Flower fresh
Starting anew
Cleansing breath
Life unfurls

Solid mountain
grounded deep
So safe sinking
back into earth

Rippling water
turning still
Lake widens
in my heart

Nature surround
Pigeon caws
Seeing within
dark mud

Steam rising
from still lake
Angst decomposing
elements reforming

Nothing there
to hold on to
Worry disintegrates
Water back to clouds

Letting go
of my notions
Mud nurtures lotus
I hold my pain

Thay inside
Breathes, Sits
Focus energy
helping now

Space free
within/without
This speck of cosmos
Consciousness

16 September 2010

After doing Reiki attunements

Doing attunement
Original desire
to make all better
Smiles contented

Deepest feeling
Reconnection
Buoyant nature
floats back up

Childhood sense
that it's alright
Telling Aunt Ruthy
don't need to worry

Covered up
by disbelief
Rediscovered
still luminous

Childhood trust
heart so opened
Told just fairy tale
That's misperception

Remember passing
familiar flower smell
from before birth
old recollection

Background scenery
of this life play
Returns to bare light
Love shining through

Healing intension
to help all beings
from essence core
clearing with practice

5 October 2010

OI RETREAT

Unstone Grange together
Freshness of recent OIs
stepping into the form
Energy flows holding hands

Taking on new roles
Moving beyond to essence
Space for us to grow
sing, laugh, deepen

We are tree of practice
sapling becoming strong
Beyond identity worry
just let our roots expand

We are the Buddha
Each Dharma Teachers
within for ourselves
naturally shinning out

7 October 2010

Solid mountain
Cliff, water's edge
Waves break
sometimes over head

Sunk into earth
One with ground
A part of all
tides come and go

Flexible erosion
Transformation
Not responsible
what crashes, recedes

Accepting life as is
No need to take on
fear of storms
I can't control

Rooted in stone
vast sky surround
I am all elements
Seeing and being

21-26 October 2010

SALEMA, PORTUGAL POEMS

Round the Sagres circle
This time no wind, peace
Cobblestone touch to earth
Water and sky so big

Bob and I holding hands
Together with eternal
Openhearted pleasure
This is true happiness

Us meditating at night
warm, special joining
Sharing power symbol
Attuning Bob to energy

Focusing on Reiki symbol
Bob's view brings me insight
Such richness and connection
A part of one another, whole

*   *   *   *

Sea sculptured rocks
Green moss, red stone
Smoothed and burrowed
in nature's flowing art

Climbing back to fortress
high cliff on water's edge
Being dismantled by time
illusion of power crumbles

*   *   *   *

Leaving behind in the sea
angst no longer needed
Roles in plays released
Ocean of life reshaping

I come out so cleansed
Not same person as before
Worries washed away
Water purification

*   *   *   *

Coney Island style beach
Waves rising so high
I have to dive under
Once out, warm watching

Water crashes, mist flies
Children scream and jump
Ocean crests, roars white
Drying in sun, I smile

4 November 2010

London life
Kev, Helena, Ella
Busy years
Much to do, create

All back to school
Ella shows me the way
checks in, gets book
'You can go now, Grandma'

Kevin at Uni
Course in full swing
Anthropology, media
blending with interest

Helena to Irish prison
where martyrs hung
Magdalene Laundry women
join victims transformed

Strong family energy
Building confidence
So lovely to partake
in London together

12 November 2010

REIKI BUDDHIST INTERCONNECTION

Written for my Reiki for Buddhists course manual

Buddhist practice
of mindfully alive
Being inner Buddha
with breath and steps

Usui Sensei lay priest
Marshal arts expert
International traveller
finding Reiki in Meditation

The living Dharma
peace energy right now
Only concepts separate
from Reiki experience

Back to Mt Kurama
childhood Buddhist School
Returning to simple way
Propelled home by suffering

Fear of disrespect
is misperception
Once released
practice gains

Special gift emerges
What we have sought
Healing hands helping
which can be passed on

Not completely the same
but surely not so different
Those overlap areas
resonate pure energy

Thank you for miracle
Magic to be shared
with those who want to grow
Widening spiritual life

In healing experience
I don't want to judge
Is this Reiki or Buddha?
Sameness intertwines

Usui Mikao taught us to practice
mindfulness, meditation, precepts
We take up these gifts of grace
healing ourselves and others

Both Reiki and Buddhism
made of non-self elements
Awakening blends
into positive way

Reiki living Dharma
one of a thousand doors
Usui Sensei Satori
energy continued

Ki energy exercises
Japanese Shinto culture
Mindfulness practice
all roots of Reiki Ryoho

Compassion of teacher
coming through to us
Grateful for healing power
Warm Spiritual Opening

His practice back to Buddha
made simple in physical form
Allowing blocks to clear
align with love essence

Buddha nature within
Same nature without
Cosmos microcosm
speck of the whole

Buddha nature Reiki
Usui enlightenment
vibrating through
this body vessel

Reiki clearing
opening to being
spiritual way
to true home

Letting go of division
between Reiki and Buddhist
What if Reiki every step
Life force each breath

Usui Sensei clearly lived it
Contented smile on his face
Teaching path for self, others
Awakening us to spiritual energy

26 November 2010

I enjoy the light
Winter moon-like sun
shining through bare branches

Breathing into Hara
not completely whole
Fear mixes with Reiki

Easing through my body
Opening to perfect oneness
In vast space shame dissipates

Childhood safety feeling
trusting being part of whole
Family called it God

Growing up, too much baggage
of sin judging Father God
to free me I released link

God beyond terrible wrath
Sweet life force interconnection
I widen to you beyond names

Buddha teaches awareness
Thay Pure Land Now
What a relief to come home

Nothing left to fight, prove
Surrendering to wholeness
I enjoy the light

6 December 2010

Giving up the fight
I took on as child
to separate identity
Coming back to whole

Releasing toxic ruts
surrendering to love
Buddha nature energy
running through real life

Letting go to oneness
nature's sweet beauty
Yes, I know the feeling
and I want it back

Mind illusive creature
Not separate from body
Together they are breath
Sitting on the earth

Subject, object one
in vastness beyond tangles
So peaceful being breath
Fresh life each instant

Primal connection deep
running though decedents
When I trust the flow
I can give up the fight

10 January 2011

Great Ella adventure
holding Bob, my hands
Out on town together
Enjoying life anew

Generations connected
Such love flows between us
London wonder through Ella's eyes
brings fresh view to grandparents

Watching Thames multi-sighted
First across Millennium Bridge
Ella sees castles, America
What fun to be in her world

From Tate heights above
she draws lines of bridge
Spills her hot chocolate
Sucks soggy biscuit

Bob inspired expedition
boat ride from Tate to Tate
Ella excitement contagious
on river, underneath bridge

Says she can't believe eyes
Perspective so unimagined
surround by wavy water
Parliament castle passes

Eight bridges later depart
children all three of us
Adults return to essence
fresh with grandchild energy

Advantageous all round
Parents educational space
Surrounded generations bond
Savouring special adventure

19 January 2011

FEELINGS AND AWARENESS

After doing a led meditation to get in touch with all feelings, from Thay's book, The Blooming of a Lotus. *I remembered Sister Annabel leading us through this meditation with such powerful results.*

Feelings passing through
experiencing whole gamut
Once beyond judgement
I can recognise and smile

Pain comes in when caught
Not in feelings themselves
Part of natural emotions
It's what I attribute to them

Shouldn't be jealous
Anger's so bad
Insecurity jangles
I should do better

Want to ignore sadness
clinging family attachment
Fear knife closes heart
I smile to my old friends

Filled with love I hold you
all my life's distress
Just transient feelings
I am so much more

3 February 2011 9 March 2011

CELEBRATIONS

Cambridge Sangha so lucky
to sit at Phuoc and Phung's
on evening just before Tet
Ancestors reverently invited

Sangha Tet eve
joined by ancestors
With Phuoc, Phung
we celebrate together

Ceremony, meditation, chants
Laughter, song, sweets
Richness manifesting
as cultures intertwine

So grateful for the Presence
Collective energy multiplies
Wishing New Year happiness
by living it together

International Women's Day
with Crone sisters, long active
Aging Women's Libbers

Each finding own creative path
to female healing expression
Peaceful energy reconnection

How wondrous to sit round fire
Speak of our struggles, growth
Enjoy warm evening together

27 March 2011

Peaceful TUC march
Massive, amazing, strong
Hardworking people
respecting what we've built

Public Sector Workers
Who care for us when ill
Teach us, young and old
Fight fires, empty our bins

From Children to OAPs
Disabled people and able
Value caring for each other
above taking care of money

What delicious energy
marching through London
Voices vibrating
Feet testifying

Multicoloured signs
Handmade at schools
Union made proudly
Ancient trade banners

We walk by Parliament
spreading our message
that we need caring jobs
for healing and growth

Connecting community
of this wondrous land
in good-hearted march
So happy to take part

8 April 2011   15 April 2011

Connecting with builder friend, Aleks, creating such wonders in our house

Intermingling beyond space/time
Jewish heritage, Polish culture
I share strands with Aleks

Allowing peace to re-surface
shine beyond such dark clouds
Blocks cover true consciousness

Contributing our stories
leaving for better life
connects back to Poland

Land that I never visited
feeling there's nothing left
New generations come to me

Magezis Russian connection
gentiles save from Czar's army
Later border shifts to Poland

Ancestors reside in bones
Love and fear in marrow
Beyond atrocities wells hope

We are much more than past
Choosing what to highlight
Centuries of our intermingling

BEAUTIFUL NEW KITCHEN

Aleks' genius
in finished kitchen
done so right

Energy of smile
sweat and hard work
Enjoyment of focus

Camaraderie
Doing what he wants
brings best results for all

23 April 2011

My dear Aunt Ruty
Remembering good times
You telling me at Hopatcong
That beauty was in the smile

All those family visits
when you gave me attention
Talking, being together
I naturally felt valued

Down to earth ways
that rippled through my life
Your advice to buy
rather than rent house

Your homey phone calls
when I settled abroad
You in patio sun
Me in night-time kitchen

Suddenly we're back in Brooklyn
talking with great ease
That warm familiar sound
The love I know we share

So much affection
and such a big hug
You'll always be with me
My dear Aunt Ruty

27 April 2011

Healing through illness
Heaps of used tissues
Rounds of coughing fits
bringing up thick phlegm

Recovery gratitude
stable shallow breaths
Fresh spring air
moving on to new day

Pacing myself
Energy low
Insights wide
Drop of whole

Reiki heal me
Buddha teach me
Beyond 'me' phantom
There is this flow

Breaking through
thought diversions
in need to let go
to release hip pain

There I see Bob
taking care of me
Dear life partner
gentle, understanding

Hawthorn flower reality
Sweet love with Bob
Growing up together
We can savour old age

3 May 2011

OI GATHERING AT ASCOT PRIORY

Being water of wave
with sisters, brothers
OI and aspirants
Flowing ocean together

Journey guided by Thay
Fourteen Mindful Trainings
Taking that road in the world
Gathering to support each other

Numbers grow to massive circle
Seniors to baby Winifred
Deepening, widening, healing
laughing and singing together

Rubbing up against individuals
smoothes down our rough edges
Dedication to live the practice
helps us through to new growth

Sunshine and dark convent halls
Footsteps of focus, in and out
Chapel stone warn by use
Soft moss springs anew

Holding hands with one another
Separating, back to own lives
Droplets of Thay in vast sea
Being the water in the wave

9 May 2011   10 May 2011

Written on holiday with Bob in St Ives, Cornwall

Barbara Hepworth garden
Sculptures flowing through
Round, pierced and angled
Large, flat and tall

Feeling widening beauty
Admiring mother of four
Works opening heart
Natural plant surround

Resonating with earth's contours
Standing stones, rocks, hills
Wondrous female sculptor
Being the landscape herself

Watching clouds
to finish painting
Seeing colours
Vivid beauty

Walk on cliffs
Wild flowers galore
Pink, purple, blue bells
even blossom through stone

White waves against
black solid rock
Rolling in formation
onto soft sand

Wind blows
We bundle
Hand in hand
Bob, I stroll

11 May 2011   15 May 2011

Connecting with Merry Maidens near St Ives

Route to old standing stones   In safe harbour of heart
Buses, narrow road   turquoise waters run clear
hedgerows flowering   Down to ancient granite
yellow, purple, blue   Merry Maidens deep

What I seek is already here   There unconditioned
So I walk enjoying beauty   natural energy flow
ancient ferns, country smells   Kind, nurturing, stable
Suddenly stones spotted   Back to such oneness
I clamber over fence
                                      Here I want to resonate
Now I touch kind solidity   Building habit strong
Grounded nurturing, ease letting go   Hearing, seeing clear
Such nice feeling, Mom's serenity   beauty of vivid life
Love is way, lighten heart
So free being timeless nature

25 May 2011

Consciousness free
from birth and death
Conditions come together
then they move on

Working with client's
energy blocks
Releasing to waves again
Pain letting go

Bedridden mind growth
Touching shrunk skeleton
Bones so light, vulnerable
Fear, confusion passing through

Thankful to Reiki force
supporting pain release
Lesson beyond hurt
Life stream flows

Giving treatments teaches me
Consciousness, different angles
We discuss change, acceptance
Reiki light pours through us

Seeing in-breath's just condition
from ancestors to the universe
Lungs, trees, non-crash, food
web in concert, unique moment

6 June 2011

***What a blessing to go with my daughter,
Kerin, and my granddaughter, Sophie, to
another Family Retreat***

Playfully Together
New Barn Retreat
Bonding in flow
Fivefold Sangha

Monastics, lay adults
childhood energy
Piercing illusion
into beauty expanse

Intergenerational
challenges, growth
Awareness spreading
healing freedom

Watering flowers
of deep connections
Roots intertwined
in field of wild plants

Blessings overflowing
Phap Vu's vivid insights
Phap Son's warm heart
Phap Nang's steady practice

Working as family
All pitching in
Cooking, feeding pigs
sharing speech, silence

Children as teachers
showing us the way
to be our true selves
Playfully Together

22 June 2011

I wrote this for a student who was coming to discuss taking the Reiki Master Teacher course

Master Teacher growing
Accepting Imperfection
Safe since beginningless time
Whole in vast universe

Resting in energy
Fear distraction visits
Smiling, coming back
to mindfulness again

Earthed each step
Power Symbol below
Harmony resonating
Watching mind spin

Seeing judgement, trying
Giving old friends Reiki
Living present now
Embracing anger, worry

Oneness assurance
Holding heart fear
in warm, soft arms
of interconnection

True to way, being
Healing, teaching
Staying with Usui
slowly blossoming

Flower of compassion
such beauty, kindness
Blooming toward self
naturally spreads roots

Being inner Buddha
Presence staying longer
Drifting out and back
Enjoying Reiki life

29 June 2011

Written for Reiki Master Teacher Manual

Reiki Master step
into great light
There all along
Shining below

Spiritual practice first
Teaching then follows
Healing, growth
first priority

Energy profound
Usui Sensei's smile
Eyes piercing kind
through generations

Focus in present
Mindfulness key
Oneness connection
Reiki flows deep

Respect for ourselves
Respect for students
Careful with our words
to teach without dogma

This life practice
healthy and warm
Taking our time
harmony, compassion

Following Reiki way
allowing it to lead
Ease without trying
Being resonation

8 July 2011   25 July 2011

SUMMER IN THE GARDEN

After heat of day   Garden Heaven
rain predicted   Doing nothing
Sweaty hope   Lying back on earth
for cooling down   Touching soft grass

Waiting for rain   Wind ripples leaves
as thunder roars   Buds blossom pink
Mist turns to drops   Nature spreads way
Lightening flashes   I watch contented

Trickle from leaves   Under wide branches
Rhythmic drip   of berry filled tree
Power increases   Breathing, chanting
Drumming begins   Garden Heaven

Rushing streams
pound dry earth
Massive release
washes clean

29 July 2011

Miro with Kevin
family tradition
Museum enjoy
connecting together

Colours bright
Painting flows
Doodle shapes
Coming alive

Sharing favourites
Seeing more deeply
Kevin's rich blue
with white sweep

My branches sway
Miro still on farm
There as we stare
scene movement

Warmth of hugs
arms wrapped round
Intergenerational
energy of love

Oh, how special
communing interests
Kev's e-book vision
for digital future

So much on
busy juggling
teaching, Uni
his own family

Feeling blessed
for special time
Walking London
sharing our lives

2 August 2011

Identity Unfixed
Elements in flux
'My' story
is just that

Unhooking need
to stay same idea
Shifting angle view
to allow change

Connecting with Dad
Holding hands in gut
Healing release
to loving us both

Getting more comfy
Letting go of 'shoulds'
Accepting myself
'as is' right now

Flowing with ever change
of shifting combinations
of elements in new ways
into what's called 'Joy'

All elements within
mirrored without
Actually the same
in varying proportions

Being one with Mother Nature
Unconditionally welcomed
Tender presence opens
Wide wings of freedom

Suddenly kind of scary
Retreating to bed
Bursting into laughter
cause this is what I wanted

Breathing
Holding heart
Dear Bob enters
'Let's have lunch'

10 August 2011

Coming together
on seesaw of laughter
Sharing sweet cakes
Being ourselves
Connecting as family

Three generations
of Florence, Marty young
Each doing well
in their own way
Intertwined with love

Sophie and Ella
growing so strong
Powerful girls
with own minds
Mazel for us all

Mishpocheh brocheh
for wellness, stability
Kerin and Kevin
sturdy descendents
on positive routes

Savouring *naches*
of luscious family
Sweeter than cakes
Such precious lives
Coming together

14 August 2011

Sophie holiday
brings family together
Cousins in London
growing up sharing

Kevin, Helena
fun with the girls
Back in Cambridge
Bike rides begin

Bob and Sophie
Cycling buddies
He shows her the way
through fens to the lock

Exploring together
Fen Ditton
Bates Bite Lock
on to Horningsea

Sophie with Cat
Daughter and Mum
At her flat
and on to shops

Such strong connection
steady granddaughter
My heart opens
with her on my lap

Love you, too
She tells her Mum
as they part
till next week

SUMMER ON THE COMMON

Passing the cows
on Stourbridge Common
Cattle to be exact
Some wide, others horned

Clumped together
under shade tree
Seeking group comfort
some jockey for place

A few overspill
onto foot path
Leaving excretions
beyond any shame

Cyclist come by
skirting the edge
Tourists stop for photos
Some wait in fear

Accompanying young Mum
worried that they fight
and her pushing pram
with such valued cargo

Passing livestock in wonder
what ease to just be
Grazing all summer
in nature's balance

Keeping grass low
replenishing earth
So worry free
with no thought of future

Back again I come
onto sunny bench
Water ripples sparkle
Kids pass, faces painted

Council Play Boat
parked nearby
Summer holidays
for a couple more weeks

6 September 2011

ANCESTORS WANT ME HAPPY

Aimlessness
beyond judgement
Hearing sound of breath
wind in and out

I want to be this
simple, clear, empty
Body pain arises
noticed, slowly softens

Such misperceptions
surrounding existence
Dense, heavy darkness
many centuries old

Surprised, seeing colour
lightness of vivid clarity
Remembering once again
ancestors want me happy

I've been told straight out
that's how to shift suffering
Countless generations
prejudice, fear, worry

Watching your back
assaulted from front
Survival at stake
guilt when you do

Running away
hiding, shaving hair
From behind barbed wire
gaunt faces, wide eyes

Skeletons piled high
just before my birth
Old connection to the Shtetl
What would they think of me?

Coming loose of fear
lingering in background
So used to, hardly notice
But haunting at night

Returning to message
they sent me so plainly
Transforming for them
who just want I should be happy

So please help, dear ancestors
I know your strength's within
To focus on clearing breath
Ease of safe beauty

7 September 2011

Reconciliation within
process so slow, delicate
Difficult and yet so easy
when I let go and trust

Hours of non-sleep watching breath
Enjoying the process for a while
growing from doing meditation
Then finding that ball of resistance

A lifetime of keeping hold
Ego or self preservation
Unpleasant dreams
Better stay in control

Not wanting to be swallowed up
Could speculate, but don't know by what
Starting before I can remember
I forgot how to naturally fall asleep

Yet innate impulse is still there
I work with past habit fear
of sleepless, uncomfortable night
Releasing that link's a good start

Feeling so hopeful last evening
Relaxed when I went into bed
And yet I was up for so long
finally reverting to body sweeps

Thank you, Phung, for working with me
over time to help with process
Acupuncture's such support
to find way back to natural state

7 October 2011   15 October 2011

On holiday with Bob in Salema, Portugal

Layers of time   International Algarve
rise up as stone   Valley pioneers
Sea gulls squawk   English, Dutch, German
There is only now   French and now Polish

Dark red slabs   Starting in caravans
freed from cliffs   later homes of wood
Waves'll lick you   Agricultural holdings
back to pulp   bought up to settle

Fine sand feel   Planting trees, raising kids
between fingers   some sent to local schools
Gentle roar   Interweaving with Portuguese
Ocean sooths   Artists showing together

Turquoise waters   Yoga teachers and builders
inviting home   Artisans, writers, farmers
Familiar comfort   waitresses, sellers, seekers
on Salema Beach   musicians, cleaners, surfers

                                 Meeting in local cafes
                                 Learning Portuguese
                                 Connecting with tourists
                                 International Algarve

LETTING GO IN SALEMA

Pick and mix Jewish
So many different things
Turkic across from Asia
Tribes up from Middle East

Diaspora my nation
Yiddish civilization
Been so many places
Tasting, so I can pick

Yiddish words now suppressed
Singsong intonation smoothed
Jokes others don't understand
Hand motions too big for England

Oy Gevalt, where are you?
Still humming Jewish tunes
Down so deep I can't hear
Come on up, so we can dance

Authentic Humming
Melodies unfold
Creative singsong
Rising in warmth

Playing in sand
as waves lap
After swim fun
in turquoise sea
Return journey
so much softer
Inspired, refreshed
Batteries charged

Bob and I
reconnected
Hearts so wide
Back to skin touch

Understanding
each other's weakness
Vulnerabilities
So sacred in love

3 November 2011

Inspired by Order of Interbeing Retreat, New Barn Being Peace Centre

All part of landscape
brown fields and green
Sheep grazing, wild horses
Earth solid, ground bare

Mud filled indents
Wet grass drying
Sun clearing mind
Warm, warm to heart

Storm past
Turmoil deep
Transformation
All part of process

*   *   *

Wandering the landscape
Changing as I stroll
Hilltop panorama
of patchwork fields

Down slope to wood
Across to hidden green
Secret tree surround
Leaves already turning

Dream sense recalled
Cows, horses graze
Freely intermingled
with birdsong, silence

Sculptured earth, wood
coexist so well
Harmony of life
resonates all round

*   *   *

Landscape visions
Foreground and mid
Background sky
vast and wide

Earth stepping here
Feet connect deep
Watching for puddles
keeps my socks dry

Patchwork mid-scape
draws me away
Wild horse
runs in a field

Distraction
Old spin
Energy leak
I come back

Standing solid
Watching nature
Interplay
green and brown

Exploring my landscape
Aspects so wide
Rolling hill beauty
Boundless sky

Beyond judgement
Sight clears
Parts interflow
Bigness opens heart

*   *   *

Patchwork vista
oh, so varied
Resonates
as my mind

One field green
growth so fresh
New ploughed soil
nurtures seeds

Small winding forest
Trees touching sky
Wild horse
scattered energy

Satisfied cows
munch in meadow
Deep digestion
chewing cud

Over time
fields rotated
Yet valleys drain water
and hills still give view

*   *   *

Fog of fear
rolls across
Outlook obscured
Perspective blocked

Emotions rise, fall
as countryside rolls
Hurt gorged cavern
embraced by soft hills

Awareness brings flow
Tears come as rain
Washing away notions
sparks insight lighting

Compassionate sun
slowly burns fog
Vista clearing
As we share

*   *   *

Sangha landscape
Each of us field
Skills and qualities
coalesce as more

Yes, each one
a part of whole
But why imagine
practice brings sameness

Patchwork together
creates such power
to chant, sit, cook
Meet, eat, laugh

Heart Sharing
Understanding
As trust grows
Action follows

Holding hands
across the fields
Singing, tea, poetry
All part of landscape

4 November 2011

*I sleep better after yet
another acupuncture
treatment by Phung*

Layer released
in Phung's treatment
Covering lifted
relief to let it go

Believing I can
sleep well and be
clear of mind
openhearted

Moving forward
with Phung's help
I try my best
She does the same

Childhood seeds
generations deep
slowly transforming
with practice, trust

Letting go
to be truer me
In energy balance
Layer released

14 November 2011

*Acupuncture continues to
help*

Stillness at Sangha sit
reaching place of wonder
Heart opening with ease
after Phung treatment

Beyond preoccupations
Wind-ups of them and us
Energy flow harmony
Fear passing to calm

Bell remembered friend
Wave rings through body
Back to true self home
Oh, what safety there

Letting vibration through
Opening meridians at joints
Beyond trying, allowing
just as Phung advised

Confidence building of power
to practice with deep intension
Gradual, steady direction
toward full moon within

15 November 2011

In honour of London Occupiers

Bursting greed energy bubble
Process so well underway
Fracture on the surface
Contradictions so deep

Way beyond individuals
Collective mindset strong
Retail therapy, fear on Tele
Covering natural humanity

Childhood love for all
Heart caring, laugh and cry
Being with cloud beauty
Open to seeing such shapes

Vibration still within us
that essential compassion
For family caught on edge
Homeless street wanderer

Sharing is the abundance
True society's purpose
Lifting us all to bounty
Enjoying safety we seek

Dear banker caught in need
to fill unquenchable hunger
for inner gratification
You need help to look elsewhere

What we want is free
Available in this breath
Taking autumn freshness
brought to us by cosmos

So much more to this life
when we return to what's real
That collective love vision
Bursting greed energy bubble

16 November 2011

After visiting Occupy London Stock Exchange, St Paul's

Sun Renewal
New generations
Rekindle fire
at Occupy London

Politicos, Mystics
Street people, Idealists
Living together
to build fresh way

Participatory Democracy
Meditation, Ecology
Sharing beyond greed
Shifting mindsets

Determined resistance
Reiki flows intense
to wide-eyed young woman
sharing tent with partner

Keeping warm together
Moved in to stay
Community connection
to Occupiers world wide

Reiki to head, shoulders
of homeless older woman
Meditation tent resident
getting choices beyond street

Guided to psychiatrist
to get on council list
Occupy support
food and acceptance

General Assembly meets
woman in wheelchair streams
Working groups report
spectrum of concerns

Fuel poverty links
climate and cuts
Health and Safety
pallets to lift tents

Facilitator reports
she may have to leave
To pick up grandchild
if meeting goes on long

Better Ways to Democracy
meets again a three
Info needs helpers
University schedule

Police picked off
two Occupiers last night
They return for farewell
till bail conditions changed

Intimidation clear
Not accepting fear
Meeting waves hands
sings 'We'll Meet Again'

Reminiscence touched
60s feel re-emerged
New forms freshness
Sun renewal

30 November 2011

After March and Rally on Parkers Piece, Cambridge

Public Sector Workers
March, Rally inspiring
All on strike together
Bob and I join support

Such warmth of feeling
with all those who
devote lives to help others
Now have pension threat

Community services
that we all need
under short-sighted cuts
of money before people

First time strikers
from local hospital
feeling no choice
but to speak with feet

Pushchair toddler
blowing horn
Children chant
with their parents

Elderly clapping
on march sidelines
Couple boo, 'Back to work'
Crain driver waves high

Nurse leader tells us
defending vulnerable
Pay, conditions poor
Pensions last straw

Physiotherapists
say standing up
for their, patient's needs
Walking out this time

Head teachers, students
linked up against cuts
University Occupiers
invite, support strikers

1926 General Strike
students acted as scabs
But this time different
together for justice

From Chartists to now
long protest history
Fairness helps us all
in mutual caring

1 December 2011

At kitchen table
best seats in place
Bob's Café
Occupied with love

Book chats and tea
Wondrous meals
Grandkids come by
Chopping and eating

Sticky fingers
Open laughs
Fears confided
Insights grow

Belly filling
Heart widening
Savouring special time
At kitchen table

3 December 2011

Opening to happiness
beyond fear of repayment
In nanosecond of now
glimpsing true reality

Future suffering
Stalking worry
Background noise
I can let go

I see you distractions
in so many guises
Kindly accepting
my mind as it is

Needed limitations
protection for focus
May I lovingly restrict
what I can not take on

Gratitude allowing
power of being
Vividly vibrating
with Bob in our love

He signs book proofs to me
They emanate intensity
Characters bursting forth
Past ready for rebirth

Beyond our lifespan
These creative forces
I savour this beauty
Opening to happiness

8 December 2011

I wrote this to a friend in the throws of
Menopause to share about mine, now
long past

Something mysterious
broke loose within
Slowly working its way
up to confused surface

What a jaggedy route
through power surges
and mixed emotions
with starry contemplations

Shaken down to core
Complacency released
Homeopathy, herbs
Coming into new way

Spirituality burst through
in search for direction
Seeking understanding
Cronehood emerged

Yes, it was long passage
Stormy, intense, calming
Letting go identity illusion
allowing freshness through

Sorry if this sounds harrowing
It focused kindness inward
Becoming a woman elder
Resonating more with love

So it's worth the journey
Accepting menopause process
with friends, nature's help
Flowering into new era

15 December 2011

In dark of night
Meditation heartens
Occupy inspires
freedom energy

Belief unbound
Restraints rolled off
Grey shades released
Intension power

Beyond fear
Arab spring ignites
Yemeni woman leader
Occupations bloom

Ella's Manifesto
at Bank of Ideas
Kev's protest photos
Helena's Performance Art

Breakthrough spirit
of year upcoming
Our books abound
Belief unbound

24 December 2011

Sholem Aleychem
back to nurture earth
Peace be upon you
Slant-eyed Great-grandma

From Asian Steps
across open tundra
Living with nature
Joining Ashkenazim

Allowing myself
access again to you
Beyond Shtetl ghettoes
to open land power

Dear mother ancestors
to plant life running through
this body called Joy
combining such forces

Resonate, resonate
as wind blows bush
Sea gull rides air
Tree communion

Old Star Trek feel
There's something more
Other ways to see
Encounter energy

Way before Reiki
even meditation
Something in stars
blackness and space

So few models
though Mom showed way
But I needed to find
my own access door

Now young generations
bring new inspiration
for peace and justice
resonating love

Deeply touching courage
mind settling with better sleep
My dear teacher Phung
as you say back to Buddha

Belief building
to trust inner power
from so many sources
joining to awaken

So grateful to muse
allowing disparate jell
coming through fingers
Putting words to feels

Expression release
Oh, such wonder
Beyond boundaries
being pure energy

As you intensify
firelight brightens
Growing more vivid
in greater expanse

For my family
now, ancestors
and all beings
Sholem Aleychem

30 December 2011

After celebrating Chanukah with the family

Collective warmth
Descendents surround
Chanukah lights
Darkness passing

Ancient messages
Live family tree
Ancestral scan
Kevin hug strong

Sophie and Ella
lighting *menorah*
Spinning *dradel*
Artwork together

Climbing trees
Sharing with each
Special presence
Influence connection

Mom enjoys
as does Dad
working through me
Resonating

Oh, such pleasure
Intimate kin
Interwoven
Kerin knitted in

Each own way
Opening to accept
Allowing love through
Collective warmth

3 January 2012

Finally courage/energy to pick poems for this book

Rainstorm wind
Ginger warmth
Head cold brewing
Allowing safe home

Branches sway in gusts
Deep howl resonates
Dark clouds drift
I view protected

Yesterday giving Reiki
Buddha, I face each other
Candle flame in third eye
Helping client, myself

May all beings
be safe, protected
Enjoying winter storm
with grace and ease

In timeless nothing
watching water drip
Tapping out tune
Letting go to soft bed

Wow, clouds lifting
Bright blue streak
highlighting trees
Bird soars by

Sudden sun break
shifting energy
Time to go out
Vivid communion

Sun in one eye
Moon in the other
Wind blows through
Tea back home

Surface of surge
desire to start
picking poems
So I jump in

24 January 2012

Settling into the oneness
River flows where it may
Laying back in canoe bottom
I can just drift along

Reiki clients
Book cover
Editing poems
Process to enjoy

Realisations resurface
again to be stabilized
Lost, I find myself
as bird returns to nest

From this state of being
immediate peace descends
allowing vibration through
Smiling, I savour feel

May I approach poems from here
with energy from which they came
Not just words put on page
but manifestations of life practice

www.ingramcontent.com/pod-product-compliance
Lightning Source LLC
Chambersburg PA
CBHW022024090426

42739CB00006BA/273